Because Love Welcomed Me

Jackina Stark

Copyright © 1992
College Press Publishing Company

Printed and Bound in the
United States of America
All Rights Reserved

Library of Congress Catalog Card Number: 91-77276
International Standard Book Number: 0-89900-408-3

Dedicated

to Jack and Dorothy Sublett,

my dad and mom

Contents

Acknowledgments 9

Introduction 11

Chapter One
New Beginnings 13

Chapter Two
Until We Can Not See to See 27

Chapter Three
Beyond Salvation 39

Chapter Four
"A Longing to Inquire" 55

Chapter Five
Hinder the Jailor 69

Chapter Six
Being Beautiful Doesn't Matter Much 81

Chapter Seven
Trying to Understand 93

Chapter Eight
A Kind and Healthy Way 107

Chapter Nine
The Reason the Rabbit Could Fly 117

Chapter Ten
Peace in the Middle of the Mess 129

Chapter Eleven
I Call Him Joy 145

Chapter Twelve
Those Who Cry Out Can Sing 155

Acknowledgments

Thanks to Rex Wolfe, my colleague and friend, who checks my work and tries to keep me from writing something like — "I was hospitalized in the hospital."

Thanks to my friend Pat Fancher who conceived the cover design and to my friend Terri Weisensee who designed it. Your creativity, talent and generosity bless me.

Thanks to my husband Tony who lets me type when I should be cooking.

Thanks to my daughters, Stacey and Leanne, who believe I can communicate and never stop telling me so.

Introduction

If you read the first chapter of this book, you will have an idea of why I love God so much. George Herbert's seventeenth century poem, "Love III," is a more succinct, more beautiful explanation:

> Love bade me welcome: yet my soul drew back,
>   Guilty of dust and sin.
> But quick-ey'd love, observing me grow slack
>   From my first entrance in,
> Drew nearer to me, sweetly questioning
>   If I lacked anything.
>
> A guest, I answered, worthy to be here:
>   Love said, You shall be he.

BECAUSE LOVE WELCOMED ME

I, the unkind, ungrateful? Ay my dear,
    I cannot look on thee.
Love took my hand, and smiling did reply,
    Who made the eyes but I?

Truth, Lord, but I have marred them; let my shame
    Go where it doth deserve.
And know you not, says Love, who bore the blame?
    My dear, then I will serve.
You must sit down, says Love, and taste my meat:
    So I did sit and eat.

This dialogue between the sacrificed Son of God with one, like me, who feels unworthy, is Herbert's attempt to personify the grace and love God has shown to us.

I have so very much to learn about who Christ is, but one thing I've caught a glimpse of is this love and grace. This is what motivates me: I write and lecture, because Love welcomed me. I also write and speak in order to help others see that He loves them, too. My desire is for all of us to see God better.

These chapters are essays that I have given from Alaska to Pennsylvania. All are written because "Love, bade me welcome." Because He welcomed me, I have new beginnings. Because He welcomed me, my priorities are different. Because He welcomed me, I may know God intimately. Because He welcomed me, everything in my life is different than it would have been otherwise.

He invited me in, and the implications of that are endless.

Chapter One

New Beginnings

One night shortly before my husband Tony and I moved from our first home to a newer, bigger one, I got up out of bed, pulled on my jeans and t-shirt and walked barefooted down our familiar street. As wonderful as I anticipated the days ahead to be, a happy six-year chunk of my life was over, and a brief mourning was called for. After one last look at my little world, I walked up the driveway toward the back door. Then I did something I hope no one saw. (Telling about it is weird enough, although lots of people seem to understand why I would do such a thing.) I walked over to the side of the house, pushed aside the shrubs and — hugged the house. After a minute or so, I thanked it for six wonderful, growing years, and said goodbye. Sometimes change is hard. But often change is also very much needed. A theory of counseling rests on the assumption that change is both desirable and attainable. I've needed hundreds of changes. One such change came after I'd been married for seven years.

I was still waiting to turn into a wonderful homemaker. It was not so much that I had mapped out my life and determined I would be one, I just figured I would be.

I had some fine role models. Tony's mother, although she worked for several years when her three boys were older and needed some extras, was mostly a homemaker, an amazing one. She would get up at five just to get it all done. The one detail that sticks out most to me is her starching and ironing thirty pairs of jeans a week. Happily. Lois Stark, much like the Proverbs 31 woman, is certainly one of the homemakers that helped form my image of "wonderful homemaker."

In my mind, being a homemaker involved many things: making curtains and wardrobes; cooking things that required cookbooks and spices; and visiting the sick and lost, the needy of any kind. It meant budgeting time to fit in all one's many hobbies. It meant taking care of all the errands so my husband would be relatively carefree after his hard day at the office. It meant tending vegetable and flower gardens, keeping them weed free and wildly producing. And, finally, it didn't mean just holding, loving, teaching my children and talking and laughing with them; it meant daily allotted hours of creative playing with them on a perpetually clean toyroom floor.

One day it occurred to me that not only was I not doing all of those things, I was not doing one of them. For me, being a homemaker, at least in the traditional sense (or the sense I had conjured up), was not working. So that night at the dinner table, while my good husband Tony was eating another unidentifiable object, I asked him a question that altered our lives entirely. I asked him if he thought I should go back to college and become a teacher. It really seemed to me that he had been happy enough during the last seven years, but I guess even he thought there must be a better way. The master-of-the-short-answer looked up at me with enthusiastic approval and uttered an emphatic, "Yes."

I thank God for that day. For although I feel like I've stumbled blindly through much of my life, I believe that because I have wanted His will for my life, His Spirit has directed me all along. I ran across a Proverb in my reading this summer that sort of supports my theory:

> A man's steps are directed by the Lord.
> How then can anyone understand his own way?

So although I hardly understood what I was doing, this new beginning was important for me. It affected how I would use the rest of my life. But as important as it was, the most important new beginnings I've made have been spiritual.

INITIAL CONVERSION

What would the lives of Biblical characters have been like if they had not welcomed new beginnings? Nearly every name that comes to mind has change associated with it. Saul of Tarsus may have had the most radical new beginning of all, though, when he met Jesus on the Damascus road. There is no greater change than that of unbelief to belief. For Paul, it was so significant that his whole purpose in living became producing believers instead of persecuting them.

Many of us know people whose lives changed very nearly that much when they met Jesus. I saw it up close when my mom and dad came to Him. What a change God brought about in their lives!

My dad's favorite song begins: "Years I spent in vanity and pride, caring not my Lord was crucified, knowing not it was for me He died — on Calvary." I've seen him throw his head back and sing that song with such gusto. I know how much he believes it: "Mercy there was great and grace was free. Pardon there was multiplied to me. There my burdened soul found liberty — at Calvary." This song is his testimony.

Mom's is simpler: "Amazing grace, how sweet the sound, that saved a wretch like me."

I've always said the church didn't find my parents; my parents found the church. They were desperate, and somewhere along the way, they had heard of the grace of God. So when I was nine, my parents accepted Jesus, and amazing grace transformed their burdened souls.

And we children were never again left with a babysitter on Friday evenings, standing at the window late, late at night waiting for them to come in from "partying." Never again did we lie in our beds hearing them scream jealous accusations at one another. Never did we find Dad "passed out" at a dirty kitchen table or see him standing slump-shouldered and sad in front of the dining room sideboard with the word "divorce" on his lips. Never again did we see despair.

They were truly converted. Jesus was their love and their Lord. The old ways of doing and thinking were replaced by new. I was at my grandparents' the morning my mom and dad formally gave their lives to Jesus; only my sister had the sense to go when they asked us if we wanted to be there. But I've heard about it — how they came down the aisle together, crying, Daddy sobbing, because they just couldn't help it. For it began at that moment and has continued for over thirty years — their celebration of Calvary and amazing grace.

I loved God so much for what He had done, for the difference He can make. I have always been affected by my parents' new beginning. It wasn't much later that I, too, gave my heart to God. I remember coming down that aisle to confess and accept Him — as though it were yesterday. I remember as a child of ten, sobbing out the confession a few words at a time: "I believe that Jesus is the Christ, the Son of the Living God."

I could hardly stop crying. And I wasn't crying from sadness or even from some sort of ecstasy. I don't know if I can explain it. Maybe I was crying because even my child's heart knew this was the most important statement one can make. This was the greatest of all the new beginnings I would make in a lifetime. This acknowledgment was the key to living. I knew it. Because of that confession, I was His and He was mine. At almost eleven, I didn't know all that would mean, but I cried because I knew, intuitively, it would mean everything.

REDEDICATION

You wouldn't think a girl like that would ever have a need to rededicate her life (this makes me about as sad as anything I can think of). But that ten-year-old girl grew up, and there came a day (it can never be long enough ago) she drifted away from God.

I'd have to tell you, because you wouldn't have known. I kept going to church. But one day I just wasn't very concerned anymore with reading or listening to His word, with talking with Him, and finally (the inevitable next step) with obeying His will. All the details aren't important, except to Him and to me, but we were separated — I had left Him. It seems impossible that that child who could hardly repeat the good confession because of tears could now . . . have left Him.

I was so miserable. It did not take me long to realize how very much I missed Him, and I wanted so much to be reconciled, to "come back home." I remember sitting on the back porch one day, all alone, watching it pour down rain. I was (half-thinking, half-praying) telling God (I am dramatic beyond words) that I wouldn't blame Him if he just caused lightning to come out of Heaven to strike me dead, "but," I said, with tears that looked like the rain, "with my last breath I would say, 'I love you.' "

Still as lonely and miserable as I was, I couldn't ask for forgiveness. It seemed like too much to ask — to have been His, to have known the joy of His companionship and His promises and provision, and then to have left — well, that was simply too much to ask. I would tell anyone else it wasn't too much to ask, but my heart had trouble believing what my head believed.

But the good news is far more than the grace that comes with initial conversion. I just needed to comprehend with my heart what good news is. I understood the stories Jesus told, recorded in Luke 15, intellectually. Now I would understand them emotionally.

Luke 15 — the lost sheep, the lost coin, the lost boy. I guess Jesus knew one example would not be good enough for one like me. Although for me the examples of the lost sheep and son are more intense, more convincing, even the joy of the woman who finds her lost coin adequately illustrates God's tenacious love.

I say that only because Tony and I lost (to be more accurate, I believe it was I who did the actual losing) a hundred dollar bill not long ago, and you would not believe what we went through trying to find it. Have you ever had the pleasure of transferring the contents of one plastic bag of garbage, piece by grimy piece, into another? That is only one of the disgusting things we did. We never found that bill, but we gained some insight into how the woman with the lost coin might have felt — how much she wanted that money back.

That was a bad day, but the day I lost Katy was worse. Our silver schnauzer Katy has been a companion to us for six years, and if you've ever loved a perfect dog, then you know what that means. I love her, Tony loves her, Stacey and her fiance Steve love her, Leanne and her husband Scott love her. The dog is loved.

But one night I lost her. Stacey came in from work about eight that summer evening and asked me where Katy was. I was working on something in my study and was really a little distracted and told her I didn't know. I wasn't worried. Katy doesn't have to tell me where she's going all the time; she has about six favorite places in the house. Stacey went to check all of them and came back several minutes later to tell me Katy was nowhere to be found. I decided maybe I had let her out in the backyard. After we looked for her out there, we concluded she must have squeezed through an opening in the fence, perhaps to chase the cat she's been growling at through the window for the last three years. Actually, we didn't know what happened, but somehow she was gone.

Stacey and I walked down the street, pleading for Katy to come home. We didn't care how we looked or how pitiful we sounded, we were scared. About a block away we ran into the Petersons who assured us they would be on the lookout for Katy. You could tell they felt sorry for us. Eventually Tony came in from the field where he'd been training his bird dogs and asked us why we were so upset. We told him Katy was gone, and although he tried to be cool, he jumped on his garage-sale bike and headed down the street summoning Katy with a piercing whistle. Stacey and I jumped in the car and went the other direction, hanging our heads out the window, calling "Katy" every few seconds.

Our search began to feel futile. Anybody would want Katy; we were sure someone had picked her up. She was gone, and I felt so sad and empty, too miserable even to cry. I told Stacey I would have paid one million dollars to hold her again. (Later Tony said I wouldn't have, but I would have paid a bunch. A crazy amount.)

The three of us finally headed back to the house. Stacey and I were empty-handed. On the other hand, Tony's whistle had attracted a stray terrier, two tomcats, a domesticated squirrel and a parakeet. I'm kidding, of course. The truth is he hadn't attracted anything, either. Including Katy.

We trudged into the house to rest and regroup.

Some stories have happy endings. We had barely collapsed in the living room when we heard a muffled sound coming from the study. There we found Katy locked in the closet (two feet away from where I had been working), happy out of her mind that we had finally found her. I can't imagine what we must have looked like when we saw her furry little face. Reunion is bliss!

So I understand how the shepherd felt, too. I like the way the King James Version describes his finding his lost sheep. The shepherd put the sheep over his shoulders, rejoicing. The way the words are arranged, it is hard to tell who is rejoicing — the sheep or the shepherd. I rather imagine the word "rejoicing" describes them both.

Jesus finishes this trilogy with the story of the prodigal son, a person who needs a new beginning as badly as anyone ever has. He is also a person who some might believe didn't deserve one. His brother didn't think so. Even he didn't think so. But the Father did.

King David was a prodigal son. He might have stayed in his chamber a broken man, estranged from his beloved God, if he had not reached out for the new beginning repentance always brings: "Wash me," he pleaded, "and I shall be whiter than snow." He went on to ask God to blot out his iniquities and to create for him a clean heart. He wanted a new beginning: he wanted to be restored to God, to teach transgressors God's ways, to convert sinners (Psalm 51). His grateful love — love that understood the good news of God's unfailing love — motivated him. A God who is "close to the brokenhearted and saves those who are crushed in spirit" honored his desire (Psalm 34:18).

I identify with Annie Herring's song "Too Many Times." "Too many times," she sings, "you pick me up where I fall . . . why you keep reaching out to me, is more than I can see." In the last line, she states her conclusion: "A treasure I must be." I think Jesus tried to tell us that with His three stories.

And so I know the new beginning of rededication. Finally I was able to ask. Maybe He placed me in the right place at the right time, let me hear the right words to give me courage to ask for what I could have had anytime: forgiveness and restoration.

I'll never forget that hour, more precious even than when I was ten and first adopted. It was not the only time I would rededicate my life. Every time I become aware of any sort of "turning away" on my part, and every time I see Him more clearly, I recommit myself. Those moments are as lovely and healing and changing as the first time I came to Him.

BECOMING

After several bouts with a formidable foe, my mother won her battle with smoking. She had been wanting to quit for twenty-five years. I am so glad she finally did it. My reasons are many, but they're different than they would have been when I was younger. In my child's heart, I almost thought (and I wonder why) that Mom's salvation depended on her quitting.

Finally, I got over that. Mom had accepted Jesus and loved Him utterly. That was that. So why was I so happy? One morning while I was ironing I tried to figure that out and came up with at least four good reasons.

One is because she's more peaceful. The American Cancer Society says that after not smoking for five years a long-term smoker is no more a candidate for lung cancer than a life-time non-smoker. Even after one year, chances are greatly reduced.

I'm also glad because she's more comfortable. She doesn't have to get out (or send Dad out) in below-freezing weather to buy a pack of cigarettes from a convenience store that had *better* be open. She doesn't have to fret and wish a wedding would get over so she can light a much-needed cigarette. She doesn't have to apologize for smoking to anyone who does not or can not understand.

I'm glad because of the wonderful victory Mother has gained over self, and paradoxically, for self. God helped her, but still she's at least co-victor, because God had been there to help her do it for twenty-five years. I'm so glad she finally joined efforts with Him. She is no longer being dictated to. She is now in command (or the Spirit of God in her is). She smiles just thinking of it. It's exciting. It's ultimate freedom.

My fourth reason is because of the sweet offering this victory is to God. It's like a gift. As Christians, overcoming self is always good for us, personally, but it is wonderful, also, to overcome self for God. I feel like I'm, figuratively speaking, lifting up my hands to Him, with my gift in them, saying, "Here. This is for You. I love You."

I think God is pretty proud of my mom.

An important new beginning is the challenge of overcoming and becoming. All God's children are growing in Christ, none of us grown. All of us are being perfected, none of us perfected: "He who began a good work in you will carry it on to completion until the day of Christ Jesus" (Phil. 1:6).

John Mark discovered this. He had disappointed Paul, choosing not to go with him and Barnabas to Pamphylia. This disappointed and upset Paul so much that he and Barnabas went their separate ways, Paul with Silas, Barnabas with John Mark (Acts 15:36-40). Yet, somewhere, somehow, John Mark regained Paul's favor, so much so that at the end of Paul's life in a Roman prison, he asks Timothy to come see him quickly and "get Mark and bring him with you, because he is helpful to me in my ministry" (II Tim. 4:11). Somewhere along the way, Mark had made some changes, and he and Paul began again.

The Christian life is a series of new beginnings. We all have different areas to overcome. Many come to Christ with lifetime habits of smoking, foul language, uncontrolled tempers. Some of us have lifestyles which include gluttony or idleness.

Some of us cannot trust anyone, not even God. Some of us gossip, some of us envy, some of us cause strife. Some lack tolerance or concern. Some of us are negative and pull Christian friends down and drive non-Christians away because of it.

Ask God to help you see the things you need to get rid of in your life and the things you need to add. Let's build our lives using "gold, silver, costly stone" rather than "wood, hay or straw" so that when our "work will be shown for what it is," it will be lovely (I Cor. 3:12-13).

I know sometimes we get discouraged and think wood will do fine. One night I sat straight up in bed and told Tony that I was tired of it all: tired of trying to be a better wife, a better mother, a better teacher, cook, housekeeper, a better PERSON. He calmed me right down by looking over his shoulder at me and rationally asking, "Just what is it, Jackina, that you think life is all about?" Oh, I thought, as I rolled over, I guess one thing it's about is becoming. Becoming more like Him. I decided to get some rest and get up the next day to see if I could find some gold and a costly stone or two for this structure God and I are working on.

I'm glad the Spirit caused Paul to write: "But one thing I do: Forgetting what is behind and straining toward what is ahead, I press on toward the goal to win the prize for which God has called me heavenward in Christ Jesus" (Phil 3:13-14).

That's one thing I've resolved to do, too.

Chapter Two

Until We Can Not See to See

Peggy and Virginia had climbed into the backseat, Nelda was driving, and I was riding shotgun. Glad school was out for another week, our four-woman carpool was packed into Nelda's Volkswagen and ready to split. We had no idea that, a mere two blocks away, disaster was waiting for us. Lots of people, walking and driving, were at the intersection when a car from nowhere ran into Nelda's little Bug and smashed us good. Before I even knew we were hit, my head had struck the windshield, shattering the glass into a thousand pieces.

One look at that windshield, and I went insane. By my reaction, one would think I had planned on being a model. Hardly. But I had planned on being able to walk around without alarming people. In that broken glass, I saw all that ended. I would be a monster.

I really had no time to think all that, but subconsciously, something like that must have been in my mind; otherwise nothing adequately explains what I did. Putting my hands over my face, I jumped out of the car and ran around in the confusion crying out, "Oh, my face, my face, my face." I was sure it was cut to pieces and ruined beyond what nature had already dictated.

This incident is one of the many ironies that make up my life. When they finally herded me into an ambulance and got me to the hospital and pried my hands away from my face, they discovered that not so much as a knot was on my forehead — nothing was wrong with my face. I did, however, have a completely mangled knee which probably would not have required weeks of bed rest and crutches had I not been running around on my injured leg screaming something about my face.

This is a classic case of my being concerned about one thing when I should have been concerned about another.

Being concerned about the wrong thing can be serious business. Especially in the spiritual realm. Jesus told us to make "seeking God" a priority. He urged us, "As long as it is day, we must do the work of Him who sent me. Night is coming, when no one can work" (John 9:3). The Bible is full of matter-of-fact passages that tell us what is important and that we don't have long to pursue those things. But sometimes, even we Christians get caught up into our personal world of priorities and neglect the one which should take precedence over all others.

When I can no longer "see to see" (as Emily Dickinson puts it in the last line of her poem, "I Heard a Fly Buzz — When I Died"), I want to have lived well, to have invested wisely. That's why, periodically, I examine my life to see if what I *intend* to do with the time I have here is what I *am* doing with it.

GETTING AND SPENDING

I don't think I'm very different from most people when I realize that one thing I'm doing with my life is "acquiring" and then maintaining what I have acquired. Henry David Thoreau may be one of the few exceptions (now there's an interesting fellow, chasing diving and resurfacing loons around a lake in his rowboat). It seems to me I remember reading in *Walden* that he didn't want even a rock in his house that he'd have to dust.

But, while I admire his philosophy, accumulating seems to have been part of my life since the day I got married. The acquiring was slow and pitiful the first few years, so I'll skip them and tell you about the first material possession we purchased which produced joy and pride: our brand new, gleaming white Kenmore refrigerator. I was ecstatic, mainly because of what we had lived with for the two years before the Kenmore was delivered. Our old, eye-level ice box needed defrosting every day, which wasn't as bad as it sounds, since the freezer was only big enough to hold two ice cube trays and a small package of ground beef. It was also a nuisance and an embarrassment because it would not open without some effort. We had to jerk the handle just right, and usually the thing was in the middle of the kitchen by the time we could get into it. Is it any wonder, my rapture when the new one arrived? It was so fine, and for weeks I pretended I was thirsty in the middle of the night, so I could get up and go into the kitchen to look at my new appliance and listen to it drop ice cubes.

Many years later, we bought our first new car. For fifteen years, we had driven cars that belonged in the if-you-can-get-it-off-the-lot-it's-yours category. Our zero-mileage coupe thrilled us; in fact, to say we were excited is like saying Hitler was mean. So I'm pretty sure the Lord was trying to tell me something about misplaced priorities when a dump truck belonging to a local construction company backed into my little car and scrunched its hood into the windshield. I wondered, as I sat there in utter amazement, just why a dump truck hadn't rammed my '65 Comet.

Of course, I know acquiring material possessions isn't necessarily bad. But if we aren't careful, we can lose our perspective and spend all our time longing for, looking for, working to pay for, and maintaining "things." I try to remember, among other scriptures, Matthew 6, where Jesus tells us not to worry about material things, like what to wear or even what we're going to eat or drink. He warns us about making this a priority in His parable about a man who couldn't get enough. He decided to tear down existing barns to build bigger, greater ones, so he could "take life easy, eat, drink and be merry." God was direct in His condemnation: "You fool! This very night your life will be demanded from you. Then who will get what you have prepared for yourself?" Jesus goes on to say that this is the way it will be with those of us who store up things for ourselves and are "not rich toward God" (Luke 12:16-21).

FEELING AND LOOKING GOOD

I want to feel as good as I can, so for some time another priority of mine has been physical fitness. After the girls were born, while I was still in my middle twenties, I decided I ought to take up golf. Golf sounded horribly healthy to me. Dad had taught me how to hold a club when I was a girl, and although I had hardly held a club since, I thought it couldn't be too much of a problem. I remembered Mom in her thirties playing 36 holes on a Saturday — how hard could it be? I started off in good spirits. In fact, I'd have to say I was playing fairly well. Then, on the seventh hole, it hit me. Utter exhaustion.

I turned to my companion (not even a close friend, just someone who thought she, too, should play golf) and told her with what I thought might be my last breath, that I was going to try to make it back to the club house, or my car, whichever was closest. I told her that if I didn't make it, to please send for help. I don't recall one other thing about that afternoon except that I decided that day that if I didn't do something about my physical condition, I probably would not see thirty. So I began exercising, and have recommitted to it periodically ever since.

Quite inappropriately, I am even more committed to looking as good as I can. I'm not very proud of this. "Vanity, vanity," nags my disgusted conscience. I will say this in my defense, my hangup is not altogether my fault. It's partly my dad's.

We have always lived just a couple of hours away from my parents' home. So one Saturday before the girls were born, some friends stopped by and asked us if we wanted to ride to Muskogee with them and surprise our folks. Flexible and bored, we decided, why not? However, our friends were in a hurry and had given us no notice, so we went home pretty much "come as you are." When I walked into the house to give Mom and Dad the thrill of their lives, Dad looked out from behind his paper and over his glasses, and said, "Jackina Lynn, don't you ever come home looking like that again!" I do believe he smiled, but I also believe he half meant it. There could be no reason for a child of his to look like I did that day.

Other people have been even more cruel. Ron, an old college friend of mine, is probably the worst. For more than twenty years he and his good wife, Pam, have been constantly stylish and impeccable. For one thing his hair wouldn't move in a wind tunnel. For another, neither of them sweat. Our good friends, the Fanchers, saw Ron and Pam at a soccer tournament in Tulsa and made this startling discovery. It was a hundred degrees that day, and most people were so wet they had to hold on to the bleachers to keep from sliding off. Everyone was soaked, that is everyone except Ron and Pam. People noticed. Terri, Bob and Pat's daughter and my godchild, went down to get a closer look. Her conclusion, when she returned, was that they had covered their entire bodies with Ban Roll-On.

I told Pam a long time ago that I ask little out of life except not to see Ron unless I have just walked out of a good beauty shop five minutes earlier.

For a short period of time, we worked together at the college where I teach. Fortunately, the Lord called him to California to preach after a few years. What he said one day just minutes before I was to go out and sing before a large crowd at a convention will explain my surliness: "You'll do fine, Jack, once you change clothes and put on some makeup."

I ran into him a few years later at a college

reception at yet another convention in Kentucky. You can imagine my horror when, after the briefest of greetings, he said, "Jack, you look bad." I think I laughed (suppressed hysteria working its way to the surface, no doubt). He went on to add, with some concern in his voice, "You know, around your eyes — you just don't look like you feel well." I mumbled something about a sore throat and not sleeping well the night before, but wished later that I had rebounded with a simple, "You smell bad." That would have been sour grapes, of course, since people who don't sweat don't generally smell bad either.

So because of the likes of Dad and Ron, I try to look my best. Actually that does seem like a worthwhile enough thing to give some time and money to. After all, wherever I go, I represent God — not just myself. Nevertheless, there is a point where it becomes too much a priority. Besides, there is a certain futility in worrying about it much. My long-time beauty operator, Stevie, reminded me of that fact the day she suggested I not grow my hair out a certain way because it would "drag my face down." DRAG MY FACE DOWN! So — this is what it has come to.

God's Word can be as brutal as Stevie ever thought about being. A scripture not on my memory list reminds us that outwardly we're "wasting away." So we should fix our eyes on the unseen, not the seen for "what is seen is temporary, but what is unseen is eternal" (II Cor. 4:16-18).

WORKING

Finally a priority of mine is my career, or my job. I teach, and, therefore, spend a good deal of time reading, planning, delivering, grading, motivating. I also lecture and write. That, too, takes time.

Rex, my fellow teacher and ex-office mate, used to make my job more difficult than it needed to be. We once had to share an extension, and he often took calls for me and would assure anyone who wanted me to come speak that I would probably be more than glad to do it. One day I told him he needed to quit being so generous with *my* time — what was he trying to do, anyway, kill me? The next week I found this p.s. on a message Rex the comedian had left on my desk:

> You just got a telephone call from Zimbabwa, South Africa, to lead a combination women's seminar and backpack tour for five months. Your topic is "The Role of the Christian Woman in a Bigamist Culture." I told them yes.

Well, I was able to get out of that, but still I give a lot to my job. Most of us do, and most need to make sure our jobs don't consume too much of us. Jobs have that potential.

Even the job of homemaker does. I have friends who amaze me. The two I'm thinking of haven't lost their perspective, but they are so good at what they do it must have been hard not to. One called just needing to talk several years ago. My thirty-year-old friend was depressed because she had just figured out that if she lived to be eighty and cooked three meals a day, there still wouldn't be enough time to prepare all the different dishes she'd like to make (even while we were speaking, I was fixing one of two meals I cook — which is why I hung up on her).

My other friend I'm thinking of is Pam, the sweatless one. She has cute things over every square inch of her house. These things are particularly annoying because she has *made* them and she always keeps them dust free. An old sled that belonged to someone in the family lies against the fireplace. It is not only repaired and refinished, but it has an inviting nature scene painted on it. (I would have thrown that thing against the fireplace just like it was and called it primitive.) She has even made her daughter, Brett, a beautiful quilt which she uses for a bedspread. (It is my belief that no one under seventy should be able to quilt.)

Although these friends do not let their homemaking consume them, there are homemakers who do. For some, nothing else is very important — sometimes, even the people they are "making" it for. Anyone with a job is in danger of doing the same thing. Being conscientious and dedicated is one thing, but losing our perspective and letting it be everything to us is another. Some careers do consume us. Some offer power and prestige, fame and fortune, and self-satisfaction, but these become meaningless when that "appointed time to die" comes. When my job becomes too important, I hear Jesus ask: "What good will it be for a man if he gains the whole world, yet forfeits his soul? Or what can a man give in exchange for his soul?" (Matt. 16:26).

SEEKING GOD

Repeatedly, scripture reminds us that life here is brief and only a prelude to that which is immortal. Yet, too often, everything else in our lives takes precedence over Christ and His church; things spiritual are accidently shoved to the perimeter of our hearts and minds. For some, after a while, they may be forgotten altogether.

I don't want to be an Esau trading away my birthright for a bowl of porridge. I want to remember what is most important: this "seeking first" the kingdom of God — knowing, loving and serving God and man. No other priority will make our lives peaceful and meaningful; no other priority will prepare us for the glory to come.

Chapter Three

Beyond Salvation

Seven or eight of us were playing Mind Game, and I knew I was the only one with the right answer — just move me up one space. The object is to guess how a person will answer a question, and I was certain that Leanne would not say the most traumatic experience of her life was getting her driver's license, receiving her first kiss, or graduating from high school. Her mother knew that nothing was more traumatic for her than the first day of school.

I know Leanne very well. I don't think I ever missed when it was her turn to answer. Leanne had made the statement years before that she thought it was nice that the four of us know what the others will say in certain situations. There's great joy in knowing another person intimately.

That's one of the things Paul prays for in the first chapter of Ephesians. He prays that we'll do more than believe in and accept Jesus — although that does seal us with His Spirit, putting His stamp of ownership on us. But He wants us to go deeper in our relationship with God, seeking wisdom and enlightenment, so that we might know God better (Eph. 1:13-23).

KNOWING BETTER

What does it mean to know someone better? My ability to guess all of Leanne's answers correctly is an example of a knowledge of one another that comes from hours and hours of being together. As the years pass and the times of our lives accumulate, I have come to know my husband and daughters better and better.

I'm like most wives who have been married for twenty-five years and happily married for a good many of those years. I know my husband like no one else knows him. In fact, most people would have no clue about the Tony that the girls and I know.

In *Framing a Rainbow* I told about an incident that made Tony laugh out loud. I exaggerated somewhat when I said it was only the second time in his life that he had done that — Tony does laugh. Quite a bit, really. He laughs at my younger brother Lance who believes eternally (and calls long distance before any scheduled match to warn him) that he will beat Tony at golf the next time.

He also laughs any night we sit down to play Trivial Pursuit with our good friends Bob and Pat, because Pat and I always say with uncommon goodwill after a zillion losses, "Tonight, we win." He thinks it's funny that he and Bob have to answer, "Who was the first president of the United States," while Pat and I have to answer, "What did Stan, the first Spanish dog ever fitted with contact lenses, not see the day after his fitting?" He chortles when after fifteen minutes of deliberation Pat and I decide maybe he saw his food dish. He guffaws when the answer turns out to be that Stan the Spanish dog did not see "the car that killed him!" That question was only slightly preferable to the one that asked how many holes a fellow in England had to put in his head with a power drill before he succeeded in killing himself. (Would you have guessed six?)

People who would be shocked to find out Tony laughs, might be even more surprised to know that occasionally he cries. Not often, though. Except for *Old Yeller*, a book or movie usually can't do it. When we were first married, we watched a movie on television called *Back Street*, with Susan Hayworth and John Gavin. At the end, with his last breath, a dying-from-a-car-wreck John whispers goodbye to Susan. I sat on the couch about to float away from my tears and looked across the room at Tony, who was totally unaffected. I couldn't believe he wasn't at least sniffing. When I questioned him about his heartlessness, he told me he didn't think it was sad. John and Susan had made some bad choices, including adultery, and tragedy could pretty much be expected.

I was amazed.

But through the years, he has become more and more sensitive, and several movies have made him sad. He at least sympathized with me when he had to blot me up at the end of *Dances With Wolves*.

I have learned there is one thing that will make Tony cry. That is loss. Of course, anyone would expect tears at a dad's funeral. On the other hand, Tony and his two brothers are pretty stoic. So I did expect deep sadness, but not necessarily tears. After years of marriage, this was another moment of "knowing better." All three of Mr. Stark's sons sat side by side facing their father's casket, buried their faces in their hands, and sobbed for what seemed like hours.

I also know what makes Tony angry. Not much — about the same number of things that make him cry. Once he hit a ball off the fairway and into the rough for the sixth time (too bad Lance wasn't with him), lost control of his senses, and burst out with the expletive, "Thunder!" Stacey heard him say the same thing one dreadful day when he smashed his thumb with a hammer. This is Tony in an uproar.

I'm sorry to say one of the few things that can make Tony really mad is me. I don't know how to explain it except to say that I can be very obnoxious. Before we got married, he told me he would never hit me if I didn't hit him. I haven't. But I am ashamed to say that sometimes I talk loudly and slam things.

He has learned to take this in his stride, knowing it has more to do with me, than him. One day, however, I went too far. Tony and I had a rare disagreement about the girls. He didn't think they had to go to the church softball game since they didn't play ball. I, on the other hand, thought they could go and at least be supportive. Why I got so ticked, I do not know, but I finally stomped out of the house to run an errand and slammed the door to the carport as hard as I could. I was shocked as I looked up and saw Tony standing in the doorway shouting every bit as loudly as I had, "I can slam a door, too!" Then he proved it. Inside the girls started crying. I'm sure they would have preferred to be in the middle of Armageddon rather than in a living room with their father angry.

So. I can make him angry, and I'm sorry. It doesn't happen much in our old age.

I know how he thinks. This is one of the things I love most about him. He thinks wisely. He thinks kindly. He thinks fairly.

For instance, I've been blessed by the way he looks at the accumulated imperfections in our marriage. I just told you about how I've made him angry and how bad I feel about it. That's only one of many regrets I have. How I envy people who come to the end of their lives and say they have no regrets. How can that be?

We couldn't have had a perfect marriage. I was in it. I was nineteen when I got married, but not over fifteen emotionally. I was as ready to be married and make someone happy as George Beverly Shea is ready to be the lead singer of Stryper. I was such a baby. I'll prove that easily enough with just one example — in order to show you how Tony thinks.

We had little money when we were first married, but we saved enough to buy some cute little pink, sheer, dotted-swiss curtains for Stacey's nursery. I loved those curtains, and I could not wait to put them up. Or to have Tony put them up.

He came home after work and decided to get the job done. He's not perfect, which is why he used Stacey's toybox instead of a step ladder to put up the rod. Unfortunately, I had laid one of the sweet pink curtains there, and somehow he stepped on it and tore it. I can hardly stand remembering what happened after I heard that dreadful rip. I cried.

I did. I walked out of the room and cried.

The next thing that happened is worse, in a way. After I collected myself somewhat, I walked back down the hall to find Tony and that miserable curtain. When I looked in our bedroom, he was sitting on the side of the bed with my sewing basket, a wedding gift which had never been used. (I barely knew how to thread a needle.) Tony not only threaded it, but he sat there patiently sewing up the tear and doing a good job of it. He looked up at me and didn't say a word. Not a "What a baby you are!" Not a "That's the thanks I get for helping?" Not a "You could have sewn it yourself, you know." He just looked at me and showed me it was fixed. Then he hung it.

That's one of my minor regrets. I was probably thinking of things like that during a walk we took one night after we'd been married almost twenty years. I was in one of my pensive moods. I told him I wished we could start again and do some things better. I told him it seems like the first years of marriage should be the best, but for us they were the hardest, and I hated that. He listened patiently enough, and he understood what I was saying, but he thought I was silly to think the first years would be the best, even though that was true enough for some. He said the years we were in now and the ones coming up were bound to be the best. And as for yesterday, it was fine, more than fine, because somehow yesterday managed to bring us to a very nice today. He won't regret the past, he surely won't be tormented by it, he won't even glory in it. He appreciates the past, and that's about all. That's how he thinks.

I also know what Tony needs. I hate to say "Not much" again. But the truth is, he is extremely low maintenance. He does have a few needs, however. He needs the table cleaned off. He needs me never to tell him what he's thinking. And he needs an ironed shirt every day. So every night I iron one. And if I had not given up saying what he thinks, I'd tell you he gets in his truck and heads off to work every morning thinking he looks pretty fine in his starched white shirt.

I know what to expect of him. He's a hard worker who has always done more than his 50/50 without commenting on the fact. I can also expect him to listen and be fair. It sounds like I think he's perfect, but there have been times when he has needed to change something, and he listens to what I say. But what I've come to expect as much as anything is his keen sense of balance. This balanced man has time for church, for work, for hunting and fishing, and for his family and friends.

He makes time for those things because they are the things he values most. It took me a while to learn how much he values time to hunt and fish, with the "boys" or even by himself. I began feeling bad because I don't share Tony's love of hunting. A good woman, I reasoned, would desire to get up at four on a freezing morning to trudge through fields with her man for six or eight hours in search of game. I had probably been reading an article about the importance of doing things together as a couple. One night I could stand it no longer. As Tony tried to go to sleep, I did the tossing and turning bit — trying to get up the nerve to ask him if he had been harboring dissatisfaction in his heart because his wife didn't want to hunt with him. Finally, I just spit it out: "Tony. . . ." He rolled over, looking for me in the dark next to him. "I need to ask you a question. Do you wish I were the kind of wife who would get up early and go hunting with you?"

I held my breath, waiting for and dreading his answer.

He sounded genuinely puzzled when he asked a two word question of his own: "What for?"

I have seldom been so happy. The next morning when he whistled his way to his truck in the frosty dark, I snuggled in for three hours more sleep under the electric blanket. At peace. It turns out that instead of being unhappy that he has a wife who doesn't want to hunt with him, he's happy he has a wife who has things to write, papers to grade, and speeches to give. A wife who doesn't gripe at him because he spends so much time with dogs and fish.

It is such a pleasure to know that man. But as well as I know Tony, I'm still learning about him. Sometimes he does what I don't expect. Like Valentine's Day last year. Tony never forgets a birthday or holiday, but at the same time, he doesn't exactly get wild and crazy. I can expect candy or a couple of flowers on February 14.

So he surprised me when he came in at noon and found me stretched out on the couch with my coat on. Some nut (probably me) had accidentally knocked the thermostat down to 58. I was frozen and glad to be going back to work soon. That's when Tony handed me a small package wrapped in gold paper. I looked at him suspiciously. No matter what it was, I had a feeling I was going to feel bad about the package of six Mr. Goodbars I had gotten him. I opened it carefully, trying to imagine what had possessed him. Inside was a really pretty, tasteful birthstone ring. Simple, like I would want. He doesn't do that sort of thing often. I was touched — happy even. In fact, I was surprised that the little ring could mean so much to me. I asked him why he did it. He said, "Why do you think?" I wanted more of an answer than that, so we've spent the last year asking that question and answering it. It's been fun.

That Valentine's Day reminded me that there's so much to learn about even those we love most and know best.

KNOWING GOD BETTER

That is especially true of God. We have so much to learn about Him. When we know God better, we know Him well, intimately, like I know Tony, like we can know only a few. Can you imagine knowing Him well enough to know what will make Him laugh?

Maybe of all the things we can know, this is the most subjective. We have a limited record of all Jesus said and did while He was here, most of it extremely serious reporting of extremely serious matters. Yet I am sure our gift of laughter is a part of who God is.

Buried in my heart are times I've thought I heard God laugh. I'll drag one out and tell you. I answered the door bell one morning to find a lady standing there, clipboard in hand, ready to take a survey. But the questions would wait, because she thought she recognized me. "Didn't you used to live in Webb City?" she asked. I told her that we had bought our first home (the one I hugged — which I didn't mention, of course) in that little community right outside of Joplin. She said she had come to a church there once and heard me sing. Then she leaned over and confided in me that while I was singing that morning, she felt like she had seen angels surrounding me.

"Really?" I said, hardly knowing what would be the proper response.

When she left, I went into the family room, sat down on the love seat and looked out the window into the blue sky. I was just shocked that anyone thought they saw angels anywhere around me — especially hovering there while I sang. That's when I thought God laughed. I was thinking He would find the concept pretty wild, too. I also think He laughed at my bewilderment. I sat there smiling for quite a while.

That's crazy subjective, I know, but I believe He laughs, and I'm pretty sure He laughed with me that day. I can tell you a story better than that, though. My friend, Rex, told me about a guy he knew, a brand new Christian who drove a taxi to pay his way through Bible college. This man, who hadn't known God long, sometimes passed the time waiting for customers by praying. He said sometimes he even told God jokes. He also told Rex that God laughed at every punch line — which was very accommodating since He was bound to have known the punch lines already. You won't

I have a friend, David, who tells about a passage in Job, of all places, that scripturally documents God's "playfulness." As God speaks out of the whirlwind to Job, He does ask some things that produce rather comical images. David doesn't seem to think that is an accident. He gives the example of the leviathan (crocodile). God asks Job several questions about this creature, including "Can you make a pet of him like a bird or put him on a leash for your girls" (Job 41:5). It had been awhile since I had read Job, and hardly believing what David said, I looked it up. As I read, I found another pretty funny line: "If you lay a hand on him, you will remember the struggle and never do it again" (41:8)!

There are other moments in scripture when I think God might have laughed. He might have been amused at the people who were praying for Peter when he was in prison. Rhoda, the servant girl, answers a knock at the door and is so overjoyed to see Peter that she runs back to tell everyone, leaving Peter standing outside the door. Then when she tries to tell these praying believers that Peter is at the door, they tell her she is out of her mind. I think God laughs, or at least smiles, when we are shocked by answered prayer and learn step by little step about His power and faithfulness.

I also think those who know Him well sense His laughter.

We can know with less subjectivity what makes God sad. Mainly people. God's Son wept for Lazarus or for his sisters. Maybe He felt bad about

Lazarus or for his sisters. Maybe He felt bad about returning Lazarus to the struggles of this life. Maybe He empathized with Mary and Martha's pain.

He was also sad when the Rich Young Ruler turned away from what He had to offer. He felt the same emotion as He mourned over Jerusalem; He longed to love them but they were not willing (Luke 14:34). There must be many things that make God sad.

It would be good to know, also, what makes God angry. Often people prefer not to think of God as a God who can be angry. But Jesus came to show us and to tell us who God is, and it seems clear that He can be angered. Jesus seemed angry enough when He drove the money changers out of the temple. He didn't exactly sugar-coat what He had to say to the Pharisees, the religious leaders, in the Woe chapter, either: "You are like whitewashed tombs, which look beautiful on the outside but on the inside are full of dead men's bones and everything unclean. In the same way, on the outside you appear to people as righteous but on the inside you are full of hypocrisy and wickedness" (Matt. 23:27-28).

And the Parable of the Ten Minas, recorded in Luke 19, contains the element of anger. The parable concerns the kingdom of God and our response to God's gift. It ends with something for us to think about (such is the nature of the parable): "But those enemies of mine who did not want me to be king over them — bring them here and kill them in front of me." Actually a whole group of parables could develop the thesis that God can be angry.

Ananias and Sapphira are literal proof of God's anger. What made God so angry that these two were killed on the spot? Lying to the Holy Spirit is serious (Acts 5:1-11). They should have known that God is changeless and remembered Malachi 1:13:

> When you bring injured, crippled or diseased animals and offer them as sacrifices, should I accept them from your hands?" says the Lord. "Cursed is the cheat who has an acceptable male in his flock and vows to give it, but then sacrifices a blemished animal to the Lord."

Maybe we ought to know God this well. Scripture says "great fear seized the whole church and all who heard about these events." People who know God are comforted by His mercy, warmed by His incomparable love and overwhelmed by His faithfulness. But we should also know Him well enough to know what makes Him angry. Someone wisely said, fear Him and nothing else.

What does He value? When He denounces the Pharisees in His Woe Discourse, He answers that in part: "You give a tenth of your spices — mint, dill and cummin. But you have neglected the more important matters of the law — justice, mercy and faithfulness" (Matt. 23:23). What else does He value? The Bible is very clear and thorough about that, but will we ever make the effort to find out?

Can you imagine knowing God well enough to know lists of things that will make Him laugh, to know all the things that make Him sad or angry, to know what He needs and wants, to know what we can expect of Him and to know what He values?

Learning these things is at least part of knowing Him better. But how do we learn them?

To know God better doesn't happen by wishing. Any intimate relationship requires being together. One of the main ways we can "be with" God is by reading His word. Anyone can tell you that, who has read a good letter from someone he or she cares about. I came to know my husband very well during the two years we wrote letters while we were dating but going to different colleges. One of my students reminded me of this same sort of thing not long ago. She wrote me a note saying she had just read my book, *Framing a Rainbow*, which is about teaching our children that they are loved and teaching them to know and to love God. It is filled with stories about us. It sounded like she just about devoured it. She said she loved getting to know us better by reading the book. She added that it made her think about the opportunity she sometimes neglects to get to know God better in His "book."

I have always tended to think that we get to know God best by reading His Word. And maybe that is true, but Oswald Chambers, in *My Utmost for His Highest,* points out that prayer, too, is invaluable in helping us know God better. He asks us to consider the last thing we prayed about and then questions if we were most concerned about what we asked for or about God. Were we "determined to get some gift of the Spirit or to get at God."? He reminds us that God knows what we need before we ask and suggests that the point of asking is the very thing I'm talking about: that we may "get to know God better." He says that we should keep praying so that we can gain a "perfect understanding of God Himself."

I catch myself singing snatches of that old song, "My God and I," especially the line, "We clasp our hands; our voices ring with laughter." I love the picture of that fellowship and communion. And for the times I've really sought Him — reading His word for guidance or insight or knowledge, talking with Him, and meditating on Him, the metaphors in "My God and I" take life and are reality.

Chapter Four

"A Longing to Inquire"

I'm slow to learn. At the beginning of a recent new year, I wrote this in my prayer journal:

> I believe the expression is "Here we go again."
> Here I am.
> Again.
> What will finally work? I wish I were different – not so prone to neglect important matters. Anything that doesn't have to get done, does not. It seems.
> One shirt ironed a day.
> Essays back before the next set is due.
> Toilet paper bought when the last paper towel has been torn in half.
> When will I walk three miles a day four or five times a week? Do my floor exercises daily? And more importantly spend time with God and His

Word *daily*? One day of public worship – six days of private. When? At least I read all of Leviticus. (I wonder if I should ever read that book again?) I do want to see You and hear You.

Fan the flickering, pitiful fire of that desire. I want to because I love You, and I believe in the power and truth of Your Word.

I knew I needed time to spend with God. I will never quit desiring that. I have at least an idea of what it will mean.

In "The Buried Life," Matthew Arnold says because of any number of modern problems, man has lost touch with who he is and with what life is all about. I have seen application in this poem, for many Christians. For although most have at least scraped the surface of who they are and what life is about, they still run the risk of understanding very little about themselves, God, and life. This kind of Christian often lacks, and wonders why, the "abundant life" and the "peace that passeth understanding" that Jesus offers. He is not unlike the people in Arnold's world who live the "Buried Life." Occasionally, almost as "empty" as one who has not accepted Jesus, he knows something is missing:

> But often, in the world's most crowded streets,
> But often, in the din of strife,
> There arises an unspeakable desire
> After the knowledge of our buried life;
> A thirst to spend our fire and restless force
> In tracking out our true, original course;
> A longing to inquire
> Into the mystery of this heart which beats

"A LONGING TO INQUIRE"

> So wild, so deep in us – to know
> Whence our lives come and where they go.

This Christian is so limited because he is part of the crowd that Jesus characterized as "harassed and helpless." He is possessed, like Arnold's speaker, by "distractions" and "strife." He is unbalanced. He hasn't prioritized time to spend with God, and therefore has no time for the things that will change him, like independent Bible reading and study and personal prayer and meditation. (It is estimated that only ten percent of fundamental, born-again church goers spend even ten minutes a day in Bible reading and prayer. This means we are virtually a "non-Bible reading, non-praying people.")

Often, as a result, unappealing adjectives like "empty," "bored," "depressed, "ineffective," and "helpless" describe us. But they don't when we decide to spend time with God so that our spirits can learn and stretch and grow and understand and rest. When we "seek God" (Psalm 27), and find Him, miracle of miracles, we shall have found ourselves and anything else that matters.

LONGING TO KNOW THE WORD OF GOD

My earliest childhood memory is not a very nice one. I wonder what makes something like this stick in the mind of a three-year-old? There's not a lot to the memory. I see my mom kneeling on the floor at the end of the bed looking intently at the newspaper sprawled out in front of her. I guess I wanted her attention, although I'm hesitant to interpret from such a distance. Nevertheless, I stomped my foot right into the middle of the paper she was reading.

In a reflex, no doubt, she smacked my little leg. I cried and told her I had just wanted her to tie my shoe. I made her feel really bad. Apologizing, she loved me a bit and tied my shoe.

I've about decided the reason that memory sticks with me is because while she was apologizing and while I was receiving a good deal of satisfaction from that apology and her attention, I knew I had mainly stomped my foot on her paper – to be stomping my foot. I also knew I had done something "wrong."

I'm not sure what to make of that. A guilty conscience at such a young age? I hadn't even heard of God, and I'm not sure I had heard that much about right and wrong.

I do know this much, we have a conscience. And as we grow to the age of accountability, I believe it is only an understanding of God's Word that can educate that conscience properly and completely. So reading what He has said to us not only reveals Him, as I discussed in chapter three, but it changes and matures us. The writer of Hebrews says the Word of God is "sharper than a two-edged sword" (4:12). I heard that paraphrased once this way: God's Word can be our critic, commending what's right with us and confronting what's

"A LONGING TO INQUIRE"

wrong.

Let me see if I can give you a fairly benign example of how it has confronted one of the things that is wrong with me. The Word of God has challenged my natural inclination to beach bumness. Poor Tony, who can get by on four hours of sleep a night, was appalled to find out his wife preferred fourteen. I've fought this battle with laziness all my life. I know I must have been born asleep and have wondered how I was kept awake long enough to start breathing.

One rainy morning when the girls were still little, I was making my bed. In fact, I was pulling the spread up over the pillows, when I just couldn't stand it – the rain, the girls still asleep in the other room – I got back in.

How many people would do such a thing? Pat Fancher sure wouldn't. Pat amazes me and our mutual friend, Connie. We are fascinated by Pat's boundless energy. Connie and I have never forgotten the time Pat confided in us that she had been so ill from the flu that she came home one evening after work and lay on the couch with an afghan curled around her and didn't move for thirty solid minutes. For Pat this was a near-death experience. For Connie and me, this is every evening after work. Or no one gets dinner.

I know that sometimes I go too far. Scripture has convinced me that idleness is a sin, and like all sins, it can be deadly. Parables, like the five foolish unprepared virgins who were locked out of the wedding, are great for this (Matt. 25). Paul helps confront the issue, too. All those who don't work, don't eat (II Thes. 3:11), and in Hebrews he says, "We want each of you to show this same diligence to the very end, in order to make your hope sure. We do not want you to become lazy, but to imitate those who through faith and patience inherit what has been promised" (6:11-12). And, of course, those who read with any understanding will see in the life of Jesus the complete antithesis of laziness.

Eventually, through much reading and a growing understanding of Christ, I wanted very much not to be lazy. I've been confronted about so many other things and feel myself growing, as a result. I also feel like my educated conscience is fit to guide me. I am less likely to carry around unnecessary guilt and more likely to face head-on what needs to be dealt with. Knowing what the will of God is keeps us from making false assumptions that leave us weak and ineffective, and sometimes, even devastated.

Taking time to read the Bible helps reveal God to me, challenges and changes me, and it also helps me overcome temptation. Jesus Himself overcame His great wilderness temptation with scripture He had buried in His mind and heart.

One night when my daughters Stacey and Leanne were staying with their grandparents, their grandpa read them a bedtime story. In an effort to make *The Three Bears* a little easier for his grandbabies, he updated the terminology a bit. Stacey was quite into the story, but two-year-old Leanne, who liked to go to sleep at sunset (her mother's daughter) was very sleepy and listened to the story with her hands folded over her chest and her eyes closed. In fact, my dad thought she was asleep, which is why he couldn't believe it when every single time he said, "Who's been eating my – soup," Leanne muttered, without so much as blinking her eyes, "porridge." Daddy could save the modernization for someone else; Leanne knew this story so well she could quote every word – even in her sleep.

I later thought how good it would be if I knew God's Word that well – that I could quote it in my sleep. Then it could truly come to my defense in times of temptation. It really is our sword, the "sword of the Spirit," part of the armor which can help us "stand against the devil's schemes" (Eph. 6:11-17). Know and then listen to the Word of God to make your choices.

I desire to be among the "poor in spirit." They come to His word greedily (the only time I am glad to use that adverb), aware of how little they know and how much they need to know. They consider finding God through His Word a "pearl of great price" and are willing to sacrifice the time they would spend on less important things in order to secure it.

LONGING TO PRAY

When I first started teaching at Ozark Christian

College, I had a student who struggled in a lot of different ways, including physically. I noticed right away there was something wrong with her mouth, but not wanting to stare, it took me a long time to figure out that, among other problems with her mouth, she had a front tooth missing. A young girl should not have to go around with a tooth missing, and I worried about that a lot, wondering what I could do to help her. One morning she was dropping by my office to see me about an essay, and at 9:00 I wrote my concern in my prayer journal:

> Be with her when she comes in, Father. What am I going to do about that TOOTH! What can I say to her? What are her needs? Do you want to speak through me? Love – encourage? Well, Father, sometimes I feel helpless. I do now. Please, as you probably always are, be here in this office with me.

When she left my office, I was so excited I could hardly write. I never use exclamation marks, but this day I went wild with them. Sometimes I don't have patience for a written prayer journal. But I'm glad I wrote this down. It's been a long time ago, and it's fun for me to remember how happy I was at 10:00, October 21, 1983:

> Father! You amaze me! A direct, unbelievable, immediate answer to prayer. I'm excited out of my mind!
> There she was telling me (simply because I took time just as she was leaving to look at a paper that happened to tell about an operation she had had) about how she was going to be able to get her

teeth fixed. Easy as pie. We talked and rejoiced together.
THANK YOU!
I love You beyond words.
You *were* in the office with us.

God has done it so often, revealed Himself to me in prayer. He does it for all those who pray earnestly.

A friend of mine experienced that when she lost her young minister husband to a heart disease that had made him extremely ill for a long time. One day, knowing he was dying, she prayed that God would not take her husband on that particular day, because it was their youngest son's birthday, and she didn't want him to always have that to remember. But at the same time, she also prayed that Danny would not have to suffer long. She remembers looking at the clock at 12:04 a.m. the following morning and being comforted right before she fell asleep. She was awakened shortly after 1:00 a.m. with the news that Danny had died, and Betty, with both prayers answered, was very sure of God's presence and care. God reveals Himself to be many things when we pray. How can we neglect it?

Prayer also changes and enables us. The story of Esther is a perfect example. In the beginning of chapter four of the book of Esther, Mordecai, Esther's uncle and guardian, informs her that the Jews are going to be exterminated. Mordecai implores Esther to intervene. Esther, very afraid, just does not see how she can do that. But in a few short verses, *she*, no longer her uncle, takes charge and decides to do an unthinkable thing and approach the king unsummoned on behalf of her people. There seems to be little fear in her declaration: "If I perish, I perish." What brings about such dynamic change? Prayer. Esther asks the whole Jewish nation to fast, which, traditionally in the Old Testament, prepares them for communion with God. For three days the people fast and pray. Esther changes when she becomes aware that God knows her need and that she can rely completely on Him.

He has enabled and changed me countless times, in little ways and in big ones. After being with Him, I've been able to say, "If I'm ridiculed, I'm ridiculed" or "If I'm rejected, I'm rejected."

I learned an important lesson and prayed a life-changing prayer several years ago. I had just started lecturing and had been asked to speak at a fairly large gathering. I had written the speech, and it must have been decent since it was published later in a take-home magazine, yet I was very nervous about giving it. In fact, I was experiencing a great deal of apprehension, so worked up by the time it came to walk up and give the talk, that I practically read the thing. Several people came up and said that they appreciated what I had to say, but all I wanted to do was get out of there. Although there was a main session after the workshop that I ordinarily would have attended, I got in my car and drove home. I went inside, put away my coat, marched up to my bedroom, shut the door and knelt in the dark to pray.

"A LONGING TO INQUIRE"

It was a never-to-be-forgotten prayer. I had some repenting to do. I knew why I had been so nervous and why I, as a result, had done such a poor job. I had been concerned about what people thought about me. I did not at that time have a ministry philosophy. This night on my knees I developed one. I asked God to forgive me for thinking of myself instead of the people who needed to hear something from His word. To forgive me for not remembering that that's all anyone needs. Him. I asked Him to help me care about only two things every time I speak: those I'm speaking to and the God I am speaking about.

They say people who speak should never lose the butterflies. A few butterflies supposedly make speakers better. I know what they mean. But I've lost them, and I don't care. Something changed in me that night. I got it straight. Whenever I speak, I do it for Him and for those He loves. I will prepare, and then I will get up and let God do with me and through me what He will. I don't know what to tell you, it's been almost ten years. I've spoken a lot since then, and that tension and apprehension has never returned.

He will change me in a lot of ways and enable me to do a lot of things. He will do that for any of us who pray. I believe the day shall come when I, like Esther, will be able even to say, "If I perish, I perish." Realizing God is our help and asking for it will change us from the Esther of 4:11 to the Esther of 4:16. Seriously "seeking God's face" does that.

Prayer will also help us overcome temptation. Scripture helped Jesus to overcome temptation when He began His ministry, and prayer enabled Him to overcome it during the closing hours of His ministry. So intense He sweat drops of blood, Jesus fell on His face and prayed that God would take the "cup" from Him. More than a martyr's death, this cup was an aloneness that involved a separation from His Father. The cup not only included shame and suffering, but also our sin and God's wrath. And Jesus asked for another way to redeem man. But when He learned there was no other way, He did the Father's will. As He always did.

Too few of us do the Father's will. None of us will be able to walk exactly as Jesus walked, but we can try. We can try to rid ourselves of an interest in material, impermanent things. We can try to forget how we feel, and worry about how others feel. We can strive to keep our motives pure, our attitudes kind. We can determine not to lie. We can decide not to commit adultery. We can, in short, resolve to do what is right.

And we will more likely try, and more likely succeed, if we do what Jesus did. Three times that night in the garden He prayed about a matter that would require incredible commitment. When I have prayed like that, I have overcome temptation. Seeking God in His Word and in prayer will make us able.

When we decide to make time to seek God, perhaps we'll be like Arnold's speaker who "becomes

"A LONGING TO INQUIRE"

aware of his life's flow." The last stanza of "The Buried Life" describes the joy of such a man:

> And there arrives a lull in the hot race
> Wherein he doth forever chase
> That flying and elusive shadow, rest.
> An air of coolness plays upon his face,
> And an unwonted calm pervades his breast.
> And then he thinks he knows
> The hills where his life rose,
> And the sea where it goes.

It's a lovely poem, a lovely thought. Probably Arnold didn't intend to describe the man who had sought God and found Him.

Chapter Five

Hinder the Jailor

Joe, a delightful young man from Washington state, wrote a poignant entry in a journal I assigned my writing students. It affected me so much I have read it to people often. It begins:

> While on the subject of camps, I am reminded of a adapted version of a Paul-and-Silas-in-prison skit. I played Paul. The skit was your typical boring skit. A person narrated and the actors acted out what was said. Thus, we cast out a demon, were imprisoned and freed. However, spicing the play up a bit, rather than hindering the jailor from stabbing himself by yelling, "Stop," I said, "Go ahead." I suppose you had to be there.

I sure didn't have to be there. I laughed. And I

guess a lot of people are like me, because when I read it to them, everyone seems to laugh. I think Joe thought we would, even with his disclaimer. Then came his last line:

> Any humor ends when one realizes how much the church yells "Go ahead" to a world that is destroying itself.

I felt the sting of his comment immediately. One of my prayers is that I might lead people out of desperation and destruction and into the light of God's mercy and love. I'm afraid my efforts are too sporadic and too feeble. But hoping to make a difference, I still plod on, believing in God's desire and ability to work through us. I would like to be like Paul.

I met someone a few years ago who might be a more realistic soul-winning model than Paul. Except for the fact that she intercedes constantly, she's pretty ordinary. All of us could imitate Leslie. We had a chance to talk one evening at a restaurant in Denver. I found out some neat things in the hours we spent together. Her excitement is contagious; she says there's absolutely nothing like leading someone to Christ. Let me tell you some of the good times Leslie has had.

One Halloween night, Leslie opened her door and saw "Satan" standing there. When she had told one of her daycare moms that she would babysit for her daughter that night, she had no idea that the woman would show up at her door in such a costume. The mother left her daughter with Leslie, explaining that she and her friend had hired the limo waiting for her at the curb to take them from bar to bar. Their mission for the evening was to decide whom they were going to sleep with that night.

When Leslie accepted Jesus at the age of twenty-nine, almost none of her friends were Christians. And for nine years she has made sure there are still always plenty of people in her life who need Christ. This daycare mom was just one of them. After that Halloween, Leslie invited her to go to the YMCA to exercise. While they were there, the woman confessed to Leslie that she was tired of being "used." "You know, Leslie," she sighed, "I just can't help but think there's a reason we're together."

Leslie lives for statements like that. It was time; she looked at her friend and said, "Jesus wants to be in your life."

Leslie thinks too many of us assume people don't want to hear the gospel. And that may be true for some, but Leslie knows that there are so very many who do want to hear. Who would have thought this lady would be interested?

Leslie and her friend spent time together talking about the God Leslie knows and loves. Within a month this mom gave up her Satan costume and accepted Christ. She's dating a Christian man now. Cruising bars is a thing of the past.

Nothing makes Leslie happier than bringing people to the Lord and watching the difference He makes in their lives. Six months after Leslie's own conversion, she led her first person to Christ. Her best friend and next door neighbor was awakened to spiritual need, because of the change she saw in Leslie. To begin with, Leslie dumped her wardrobe — she no longer felt comfortable wearing shorts shorter than what she was wearing underneath them or blouses that plunged to the waist. Her conversation changed, too. And her interests. She craved God's Word instead of the trashy novels she had consumed before. Her friend Cheryl noticed.

As is often the case in extremely close relationships, bringing Cheryl to Christ was no easy task. But Leslie prayed, loved, and never gave up. Eventually Cheryl and her husband did accept Christ.

About this time Leslie was providing day care in her home. Her kids came from non-Christian families, and Leslie introduced God into every conversation she could. Sometimes she was subtle, but sometimes she wasn't at all. For instance, one day when a husband and wife were picking up their child, she asked them if they would like to know how she came to Christ. Surprising enough, they said yes. Not long afterward, Leslie fixed lunch for them and told them about what Christ meant to her life. They accepted Him a couple of weeks later.

Of course, some people are not ready in a couple of weeks. But people in Leslie's life know she is there when they are ready. Colleen was a friend who was not ready for a long time, but during a family crisis, Leslie was the person she called. Leslie crawled out of bed at four in the morning and drove through a snowstorm to be with her friend. It was that morning that Colleen found God.

When Leslie gave up her day care and started teaching in a Christian school, she ran into a problem that a lot of us have. She found she was surrounded by only Christians. It bothered her so much that she actually prayed that God would bring her someone who needed Him. She had hardly said amen when the doorbell rang. There in a Denver suburb, stood an Avon lady. The woman looked at Leslie oddly. She couldn't believe she had rung the doorbell of the sister of an old high school friend. After they sat down and got comfortable, Terri asked Leslie, "What's been going on in your life?"

Maybe you know enough about Leslie by now for that to bring a smile to your face. What a lead. Leslie could never let a question like that pass. She smiled and declared: "God is blessing me." Then she fixed lunch again (she fixes lunch for people a lot). As they sat and ate and talked, a happy woman told an unhappy woman about her "Lord Jesus."

Leslie just doesn't run out of opportunities. Once after she had been taking aerobics at the YMCA for years, the Y became desperate for instructors and asked Leslie to teach. She said she would, but only (bold thing) if she could use her upbeat, contemporary Christian music. Since they needed someone so badly, they agreed. Leslie wouldn't want you to think it's always easy. She ended up being walked out on a few times, but the rewards overshadow that kind of discouragement. For she has also led three women to Christ and is in the process of teaching two others.

One evening when the aerobics class was over and the ladies were getting ready to hit the showers, one of the women said to her, "I just love your music. What kind is it?"

"Christian," Leslie told her.

The lady's face indicated she didn't understand. "Crystal?"

"Christian," Leslie repeated.

"Christian?"

A month later the same lady came up to Leslie, obviously upset. The man she had been living with had committed suicide. In despair she said, "I think I need Jesus in my life." She wasn't really ready for that commitment for several months, but Leslie was there the moment she was ready. Since then, this woman has brought others to Christ. Leslie calls herself a grandmother.

What Leslie does really isn't all that complicated. She makes acquaintances, develops friendships, loves with God's love, and tells people what she knows about Him.

We can do that. All we need is a little sensitivity, a lot of prayer, and some time. Those things aren't all that hard to come by; still most of us don't intercede.

We might do a lot of things, but not that. A minister of a large church in southern California has said that he could get his people to do about anything: drive the church bus, teach Sunday school, run the nursery, sing in the choir, but he couldn't get most of them to evangelize.

I'm not sure why, but I don't think it's because we don't know the need for it. Scripture is clear about the consequences of not accepting Christ, and if that weren't enough, the devastated lives of people without Him also demonstrate the need.

And the reason we don't evangelize can't be because we don't want to. Lots of people want to. We just must not believe people will listen and we must not know what to do. Maybe Leslie's life will help motivate us. Hopefully something will, because we need to find a way. Maybe something subjective will help motivate you. It did me.

It was a song and my reflection on it. The first time I heard it on the radio, I was dusting. It had such power that I actually quit dusting and took myself and the dust rag over to the couch to sit down until the song was over. It created such a mental image for me that it made me want more than ever to find my way to bring people to God. As I sat there listening to it, I cried just thinking about the moment when I actually would see Him:

> The sky shall unfold preparing His entrance;
> The stars shall applaud Him with thunders of praise.
> The sweet light in his eyes shall enhance those awaiting;
> We shall behold Him then face to face.

The second time I heard it, I was working in my

office at school. I heard it just faintly and leaned over and turned up the sound. This time we, the recurring pronoun in the chorus, affected me:

> We shall behold him; we shall behold him
> Face to face in all of His glory.
> We shall behold him; we shall behold him
> Face to face, our Savior and Lord.

Now tears came for a different reason. I didn't just think about me seeing Him in that moment, but as the song played, I looked at the pictures in my office and thought about the others:

We, my husband and my daughters.

We, my mom and dad.

Loren, my sister, who once sneaked into the bathroom when I was taking off my makeup, sat on the side of the bathtub crying about some heartache and running the water in the tub at the same time so Mom and Dad wouldn't hear her and worry.

We, my crazy brother Lance who once drove down a highway before it was opened, found it abruptly ran out a few short feet from entrenched railroad tracks and himself in Dad's car tettering on those tracks, barely able to get his date out before a train wisked the car several miles down the way.

Nelda, my friend all through high school, who once shocked her stuffy boyfriend at the movie theater by finding an egg in her delapidated theater seat, pulling it out, and saying, "Look what I laid, James."

We, Claudette, my old college roommate who was kind enough to tell me after I had been married a few months that Comet would get those scratches out of my battered sink. (One of several things I didn't know.) And Rick, her husband and also a college buddy, who probably shouldn't have taken days off from running his business just so he could make the long trip to Joplin in order to make our daughter a spendid video of her wedding.

My friend, Pat, who when we get too old to walk the mall, has promised to push me in a borrowed grocery cart.

My mind floods with the "we's" I could list.

We shall behold Him. All of my brothers and sisters in Christ, part of the redeemed who shall behold Him when He returns. How happy we'll be. I start quoting Revelation just thinking about it: "Even so, come, Lord Jesus!"

Except, I'm afraid, if I read scripture right, there will be so many who won't be included. Maybe we could make a list of people for whom we can intercede, so that we can pray and love them into Christ.

Stephen Crane, a young American writer at the turn of the century, grew up in a family of ministers yet somehow became an atheist. Hopefully, the picture he paints of a "typical" Christian is distorted and inaccurate and not a picture of any of us. In his novel, *Maggie*, the main character, a teenager, has been kicked out of her house and doesn't know where to go or what to do. Maggie is dirty; she has been taken advantage of; she is, in fact, a sinner. In her need (she is so needy that within the next hour she will walk down to the river and drown herself), she passes a clergyman on the street and this is what happens:

> Suddenly she came upon a stout gentleman in a silk hat and a chaste black coat, whose decorous row of buttons reached from his chin to his knees. The girl had heard of the Grace of God and she decided to approach this man.
> His beaming, chubby face was a picture of benevolence and kind-heartedness. His eyes shone good-will.
> But as the girl timidly accosted him, he gave a convulsive movement and saved his respectability by a vigorous side-step. He did not risk it to save a soul. For how was he to know that there was a soul before him that needed saving?

I wish Stephen Crane's experience would not have let him imagine such a thing. And while I don't think most of us would do this, I wondered when I read this, like when I read Joe's journal entry, what this does have to say to me.

A scene out of the first chapter of Mark is the complete antithesis of the one above. A man with leprosy came to Jesus and begged Him on his knees, "If you are willing, you can make me clean." Jesus was filled with compassion and "reached out His hand and touched the man. 'I am willing,' He said. 'Be clean.'"

I want to be like Jesus, not like the man in the chaste black coat. But I know that if I am going to be anything like the Savior who makes life whole

HINDER THE JAILOR

and good, I can not say casually or callously to the "jailor," or to the world, "Go ahead!" Instead I will be a "willing" extension of His truth and love.

Chapter Six

Being Beautiful Doesn't Matter Much

My friend Pat thinks it's ridiculous for me to call myself a beach bum. She says I work hard. And I guess it's true — sometimes I do. But I never think of my long hours in heroic terms, like I think of Pat's. When I stay up until midnight "working," I'm surely not folding clothes or ironing; I'm generally either reading or writing.

I've been known to get up early, too, at least on work day mornings. I've never been happy about getting up at 6:00. Work days always begin the same. Still half asleep, I stumble into our bathroom, grope for the light, snap it on, and glance in the mirror before I step on the scales and get into the shower.

The worst morning of my life, the ritual stopped when I glanced in the mirror. A grotesque image looked back at me. I was overcome with horror.

Then horror gave way to curiosity and a strange sort of practicality. I began to scrutinize this "thing" in the mirror to discover exactly what was wrong and how I might deal with it, before 8:00, when I had to be in the classroom.

There were two major problems: (1) I had huge, lumpy, disfiguring, oozing crater-like sores all over my face, and (2) my hair was falling out in great wads all over my head — a clump was missing over my right ear, one was gone where my bangs should have been, and another bald spot shone right in the middle of the back. More hair was missing than was not. Horror and practicality gave way to sickness and defeat. There was nothing to do here but turn out the bathroom light, go back to my bedroom, sit down in the rocker, swivel it to the wall, and wait to die.

Mom tells me that sometimes when Dad has nightmares, she hears him crying in a little voice next to her, "Wake me up, wake me up." I don't do that, or Tony would have heard my little voice early that morning. I'm happy to tell you that while I sat facing the wall, instead of dying, I woke up.

This is just another of those things I wonder about — why we dream what we dream. (Last week, for instance, I dreamed a tiny bald eagle, smaller than a humming bird, was flying through the house in slow motion.) I don't know why I dreamed about the monster woman. I might have had this dream the night after a regular search for lurking gray hair produced one. I screamed (even though Proverbs 16:31 says "gray hair is a crown of splendor"). I tried to tell Tony, who was already in bed a few feet away, about my upsetting discovery. Usually pretty patient, he cut me off short, saying, "Don't tell me your troubles. What if you were going bald?" That shut me up. It's hard to argue with his logic.

I've already confessed my priority to look my best, and if I were more honest, I'd probably say I would like to look really nice. The complete truth is, I wouldn't mind my husband thinking I were beautiful, like the man in the Song of Songs thought his lover was beautiful. In fact, I fantasize hearing Tony say such things:

> You are beautiful my darling . . . lovely as Jerusalem, majestic as troops with banners.

I really love the next two lines:

> Turn your eyes from me;
> They overwhelm me.

Actually, I'm afraid if Tony quoted any two lines, it would be the next two:

> Your hair is like a flock of goats
> descending from Gilead. (Song of Songs 6:4-5)

Maybe by the time you read this, I will have finally reached my goal of growing past this ageless, universal tendency to worry about how we look (I sometimes think of it as a 20th century American tendency, but I know that this concern has preoccupied and tormented women, and men too, beyond all boundaries).

I want to be concerned about more significant things. Harold Kushner, in his article "Biggest Mistake I Ever Made," quotes Peter Lynch, the "investment superstar who turned the Fidelity Magellan mutual fund into a $13-billion behemoth." He gave all this up to spend more time with his family, saying, "I don't know anyone who wished on his deathbed that he had spent more time at the office" (Reader's Digest, July, 1991, 71).

In the same way, I don't know anyone who wished he or she had looked nicer more often. When I die, will anyone be glad that I passed his or her way? Will I have made anyone's life better? For even though people might compliment our appearance from time to time, ultimately how we look matters very little to anyone. I doubt even one person grieves over the loss of someone who merely looked her best each day.

The people who matter to us are those who have helped us through life, in any number of possible ways. Most of us need some sort of help at one time or another. Jesus taught us to give it shortly before the Feast of the Passover, when He was to be betrayed and crucified.

He told a parable about the sheep and the goats, those who took care of the needs of mankind and those who didn't. This parable is an explanation of their judgment. Those who fed the hungry, gave a drink to the thirsty, clothed the naked, took in the stranger, and visited the sick or the imprisoned received eternal life. Those who didn't were punished. Jesus says that "whatever you did for one of the least of these brothers of mine, you did for me" (Matt. 25:31-46). Jesus wanted us to meet the needs of all of mankind just as He did. One of the most outstanding qualities of Jesus was His concern. Jesus, always busy on His way somewhere to do something, cared about men and women, and His concern, always deeper than "feeling," was marked by action:

> Jesus on a trip to Jericho concerned about an unpopular little man in a tree (Luke 19:2).
>
> Jesus concerned about the misery and isolation of ten lepers (Luke 17:11).
>
> Jesus concerned about the degrading, mixed-up life of a woman by a Samaritan well (John 4:26).
>
> Jesus concerned about the naked, demon-possessed, wild man from Gadara (Luke 8:26).

But are we willing to be a neighbor to mankind, in the Good Samaritan tradition of Luke 10, and meet needs both physical and emotional? Jesus' society was no more desperate than our own. Our great literature documents need.

In Albert Camus', *The Stranger*, the main character awaits his execution sure that "nothing,

nothing mattered." He believes himself to be a "victim" of chance, tossed about by the wind of fate, "a dark wind" that "leveled whatever was offered to him throughout his whole absurd life." Without exactly meaning to, he has killed someone, and the last sentence of the book expresses his final desire: "For everything to be consummated, for me to feel less alone, I had only to wish that there be a large crowd of spectators the day of my execution and that they greet me with cries of hate." Camus' world view is not rare. A deterministic pessimism pervades much of our literature. It is a logical result of disbelief. This hopelessness is the effect of life without God.

We hear the same pessimism in the streets and homes of every inhabited place in the world. While enjoying a lazy afternoon canoeing in a canal in Seattle, Washington, one of my former students and her cousin saw a young man jump from Aurora Bridge and knew he was trying to commit suicide, for the bridge was infamous for that reason.

They thought surely he had been successful, but they heard him moan and frantically rowed over to him. As they tugged and pulled him into the boat, he cried, "Let me die; let me die."

Unable to see the 23-year-old young man because hospital personnel thought it would be too emotionally difficult for him, the girls sent him notes and told him they were praying for him. His father came and took his son home to California, and later the young man wrote to the girls: "My body seems determined to live, so what the hell? Maybe I'll get it together and find this inward peace you call Christ."

I have wondered, as my student Laura wondered, how many people have no better reason to live than "what the hell." Such misery, of one kind or another, is all around us. We would see it if we would just open our eyes; Jesus asks us to intervene as He would.

A group of good men in a large congregation in California is an example of how we don't. The minister tells about meeting with these sixteen men in a discipling group. They studied a passage of scripture together, memorized portions of it, answered relevant application questions, and prayed. One night a study question asked them to name a person they had helped that week, in any way. Not one man could cite an instance. Even the minister said he couldn't come up with a person he had helped that was not "job" related. He encouraged them to find someone that week to love tangibly, by doing something for them. The next week when the question was asked, the results were exactly the same. I expected something different when he told the story. But this, perhaps, is the most realistic ending to the story. They were good men, taking the time to study, memorize and pray. Yet week after week, they found they were doing nothing for others.

I'm sorry to say I know how easy that is to do. I remember driving home from work one misting afternoon. There was a little touch of chill in the air, and I had a splitting headache and could not wait to sit on the couch and wrap my afghan around me (you might have guessed). As I stopped at a red light, I noticed an old man walking down the street. Actually, I guess he sort of labored down the street. But the light turned green, and in a matter of seconds, I was a few blocks closer to home. I continued driving several more blocks before I dispensed with rationalizations (such as thinking the last thing that poor man needed was my cold) and decided I had to go back and look for that old man and take him wherever he was going. But all I can say is he must have picked up speed after I passed him, because, although I drove slowly up and down street after street, I could find him nowhere. An hour later snuggled on the couch, I didn't rest very easy. It was hard to rest when I had passed up a chance to love someone like Jesus would have.

A legend about St. Francis of Assisi underlines the words Jesus spoke. Once while riding alone, Francis came upon a pitiful leper. Ordinarily he would have been sickened, even offended, by such a sight. But this time he felt something stir deep within him: he dismounted, threw his arms around the leper and drew him close. When he finally pulled away, he saw that he was not embracing a leper with countless, open, running sores; instead he was embracing Jesus. Commentator William Barclay makes this observation: "The nearer we are to suffering humanity, the nearer we are to God." This was true for St. Francis. This wealthy and influential aristocrat turned his back on all he could have had and lived a life dedicated to spreading the gospel and serving the needy. Our love for Him seems very real when we do what He has asked: "Love others as I have loved you" (John 15:12).

There are modern day saints whose lives imitate St. Francis. There are those today who are compelled by Christ in them to love others by meeting their needs.

An October 3, 1991, newspaper column by William Raspberry featured such a woman. In a "crowded and impoverished" little apartment, Dorothy Perry takes care of children who have no one else to look after them. Dorothy's five children are grown and on their own, but these other needy children (often as many as ten are there at a time) have found this woman to nurture them. The children love her because she takes time to listen to them, but she does a lot more than that:

> Her nightly schedule begins with Bible reading ("We start with Genesis at the beginning of the year, and by the end of the year, we be completed the Bible.") and may be followed, depending on the day of the week, by Gospel singing, coupon clipping, cooking, "ambition rap" ("That's where we sit around and talk about our likes and dislikes, our happy times and our sad times, what we want to do with our lives.") and always study.

She calls what she and the children share "a beautiful experience." These children with substance abuse and absentee parents have been touched by Dorothy Perry for twenty-three years.

She isn't alone on the planet. There are Christians everywhere who are making "love thy neighbor as thyself" a reality. I remember a girl in one of my classes who was influenced by her minister father and her mother because they took in a family of seven Cambodian refugees. Helping was their lifestyle. These same parents took their three children on an annual trip to the grocery store to buy food for a family who would not be having Thanksgiving dinner except for their loving concern.

Two sisters who own a dress shop have their own way of helping. They buy clothes for children who would never have new clothes otherwise.

Some people learn to care and give at a very young age. When my son-in-law Scott was dating Leanne, she told me about the evening he stopped his jeep to help a "bum." The picture of that old man in McDonald's eating a hamburger across the table from a young "friend" makes me want to kiss Scott (except he only likes Leanne to kiss him, so I will settle for affectionately rubbing the top of his head).

These people have taken in strangers, fed the hungry and clothed the naked. Except for Scott (who is exceptionally cute), I don't know whether they looked nice or not. I doubt that mattered to anyone who was helped.

I try to understand more each day that loving and caring for others is what the Christian life is about. All the law and the prophets hang on these two great commandments: love God and man with all your heart (Matt. 22:37-40).

So a few weeks ago I was in the car again, driving home from a dentist appointment on a hot summer day. Lots of cars zipped by her, and so did mine. An overweight woman hobbled down the street on crutches (this woman was clearly not a healthy hitchhiking killer tricking motorists on I-44). She had put the strap of some sort of bag around her neck to free her hands to grasp the crutches.

Although I drove by, at least this day I got only a half block before I turned around and went back. I did, however, have enough time to wonder what in the world I would say to her, to wonder how I would get her in the car, to wonder what I would do if she had nowhere to go, to wonder what those waiting for me at home would think if this took a long time, to wonder, even, if she would rather hobble down the street without my help.

When I got around the block, she had turned into a yard and was halfway between the street and the house. She turned around and looked at me as I let the automatic window down. I felt pretty stupid. "Is this your house?" I asked. She nodded her head up and down, and smiled faintly. I mumbled something about how I hadn't wanted her to have to walk on such a hot day. She looked at me just a second longer and then turned around to walk into the house.

That was a pitiful effort. But when she looked at me, I thought I looked into the eyes of Jesus. And sloppy though my attempt was, I felt more His than I had since the last time I had loved someone for Him.

It wasn't St. Francis or Dorothy Perry. And it sure wasn't Jesus. But it was a start.

Chapter Seven

Trying to Understand

The kids were making us crazy. The drive back from Tahlequah, Oklahoma, was the fitting end to our mini-vacation. All five kids were still in grade school when our friends Bob and Pat went to see the Trail of Tears play in the outdoor theater with us. We should have guessed what kind of weekend it would be when Tony and Bob checked us into our motel. It looked half decent, but let me tell you, this place will never light its No Vacancy sign.

One of the three Fancher kids came into our room with the shocking news that there was a huge hole in the ceiling of their bathroom. I was still trying to get over the fact that the red shag carpet in our room had left the floor and run a good two feet up the wall. Stacey and Leanne took advantage of my emotionally weakened state and got a quarter from me for the "magic fingers" machine on the bed. It was broken, of course. No massage, and no quarter (a bigger rip off than a juke box).

We still had two hours before dinner and the play. The red room was giving me a headache and the hole in the Fanchers' bathroom ceiling was scaring their kids, so Pat and I decided to take the kids to the pool. This pool was the reason Pat allowed the guys to stop at this motel anyway. How bad can a place with a pool be? (We now have the answer to that.) This pool wasn't much, maybe that's the real question to ask — what's the pool like? I'll say this much in its defense, it was an in-ground pool. After that, the defense rests. It was only about the size of an ice cube tray, and it was located about two feet from the highway. We could handle that; small pools with no atmosphere were not foreign to our experience. But this pool was unique in one way. When Pat and I got the five kids out of the pool to go get ready for the evening festivities, we were white. I don't know if they did or did not put formaldehyde in that pool, but we looked like escapees from biology specimen jars.

So now we were on our way home, and, as I said, the kids were driving us crazy. All they could do was complain. They weren't complaining in general. The ones in the middle seat of the Fancher station wagon, in fact, weren't complaining at all. The whining came from the three in the

TRYING TO UNDERSTAND

back area with the ice chest. They were hot. They were sweating. They coughed and grabbed their throats. And the truth is the station wagon was having trouble with the air conditioner; none of us had much cool air. After a few more wails, Pat and I decided to teach our children some important lessons. They needed to see what grace under pressure meant, and more importantly, they needed to see what it means to worry about how others feel and not how you feel all the time. So the trade was made.

I'm not sure the kids saw the beauty of our self-sacrifice, but I do know they were quiet all the rest of the way home in seats one and two. Meanwhile, Pat and I paid a high price for harmony. We tried to look cool for two hours while people drove up behind us, staring at two haggard women crammed into the back of a station wagon with their sweaty legs draped over the top of an ice chest.

Thinking of others just isn't easy to do. Maybe that's why I spent so much time working on that with my daughters. When the girls used to argue (mainly over clothes) I would seldom let it pass: "Don't you know," I'd ask, sometimes patiently, sometimes not, "that what you are saying shows a total disregard for how the other person feels and demonstrates your concern for self?" That's what fights almost always mean to me. My noble reasoning causes me a great deal of stress when I start one. But I guess that's okay, because battling self-interest is important. It is an antithesis of Christ, and I think it is a root of sin.

While the girls were growing up, I was always trying to show them the reality and effect of it. I know it starts early, this thinking of self and not being concerned about others.

One day Stacey and I were shopping at the mall and happened to pass by a fashion show put on by different shops in the mall. The "models," girls who worked in the stores, were doing their best. While we watched, Stacey nudged me and pointed out four or five high school girls who were standing on the side lines, making fun of the models. I stood there, embarrassed for the girls on the stage and for the ones being so insensitive. As we walked off, my daughter informed me that the hecklers were from one of the big churches in town and went to a Christian school. Stacey looked into my eyes for a reaction. I'm sure she expected to see disapproval there, even though these girls were young and had a lot to learn.

She found herself reacting to unkindness recently. She had gone with her youth minister fiance to a lock-in he was helping with. Standing on the sidewalk in front of the church, she saw a mother drive up with her daughter. The daughter was about to get out of the car when she saw another woman drive up with her daughter and two visitors. Stacey heard the girl in the first car say to her mother that she wasn't going to stay if those girls were coming. That shocked Stacey, but not as much as her mother's response. "I don't blame you, Honey. You don't have to stay." And she didn't. Later I heard Stacey tell her sister this story. She ended by saying, "Do you know what Mom would have said if we'd made a statement like that?"

But Stacey's mom is grown up and much further along in her Christian life, and still she does so many things to repent of. Just last spring on a trip to the inner-city with twenty college students, I sat around the table after a hard day's work and made a joke at someone's expense. The someone wasn't there, but it was such an unkind thing to do that I had to write a note to those who heard me and apologize for such insensitivity. How can those of us who know Christ be so oblivious to the little ways we hurt people? How can we so often devalue those Jesus values?

Jesus asks us to "feed his sheep," but instead we often ignore them or wound them (or even "kill" them). Observing this tendency, song writers address the problem in songs like, "Don't Let Another Wounded Soldier Die." Our prejudices, our sensibilities, our amusements, our feelings cause us to hurt others.

A young girl came down the aisle one morning to accept Christ. She knew only two people in the congregation, the ones who introduced her to Jesus. I've often thought about how frightening it must have been to come before that congregation. She knew nothing about church, really, and this one was relatively sophisticated. She was not. She was uneducated and poor, and she looked it. As she came down the aisle, I heard a woman behind me say, "Look at those skin-tight pants she has on." I think she said the girl should be ashamed.

On another Sunday morning, a young man sang a special. While he sang, my daughter heard a woman behind her say, "Oh, Lord."

Then there was the morning I found our minister's wife crying in the bathroom. Someone had just verbally attacked her husband again.

Most of us, if we'll examine our lives closely, will find that to some extent, we, too, are guilty of thinking of ourselves and not thinking of others. Here are a few generic examples:

No one cares one bit about all that I do. See how they like it when I don't do it anymore.

I do not want people clapping while I sing. I do not care if there is no scriptural precedent forbidding it, there should be.

I want to clap when I sing. I have every right to. I enjoy it. Intolerant people make me sick.

I've been teaching for twenty-five years. It's about time someone else did it for awhile. I deserve a break.

I want an apology for what he said to me. Or worse, I will accept no apology for what he said. It is unforgiveable. I didn't deserve it. I was hurt.

It begins to sound like nothing matters except what *we* want and what *we* feel. But there is something to consider that should encourage us. Maybe it shouldn't be so surprising that we are capable of such things. We can find comfort in the fact that, even after spending three years with Jesus, the disciples were capable of self-interest, too. And we can find comfort in the way Jesus confronted them when they were.

The place is the upper room where Jesus and His disciples were partaking of the "Last Supper." The time is the close of Jesus' ministry, just before His crucifixion, resurrection and ascension. Right after a most sacred moment, when Jesus broke the bread and shared the cup with His disciples, we read in Luke 22:24 what commentator William Barclay calls "the tragic sentence": "A dispute also arose among them, which of them was to be regarded as greatest."

They had argued about this before, so now Jesus did something that they surely would never forget.

Amid this collage of talk about death, betrayal, and greatness, Jesus, because He loved them and wanted to show them the "full extent of His love," took off His outer clothing, put a towel around His waist, poured water in a basin and knelt to wash His disciples' feet. When He had finished, He asked them if they understood what He had done (John 13:1-17).

Did it finally sink in? Did all they had seen and heard, in addition to all they would see in the next few days, make sense in this one moment?

From the beginning, "the Word was with God, and the Word was God," yet He "became flesh and lived for a while among us" (John 1:1-2a). He didn't say — "I don't have to do that!"

Although He was in the world, made the world, and came to those who were His, they "did not receive him" (John 1:10-11). He didn't say — "No one cares. Why should I worry about it?"

Jesus "did not consider equality with God something to be grasped, but made himself nothing, taking the very nature of a servant . . . and humbled himself and became obedient to death — even death on a cross" (Phil. 2:6-8). He didn't say — "It's not right. I don't deserve something like that."

When a ruler asked Him to come and lay His hands on his daughter who had just died so she could live, "Jesus got up and went with him" (Matt. 9:18-19). He didn't say — "I am extremely busy. I have important things to do here."

When "Jesus, tired as He was from the journey, sat down by the well" and asked the sinful Samaritan woman for a drink, she couldn't believe it. But before they were through talking, He had changed her life. He didn't say — "Do you see what that woman has on? There's nothing she hasn't done and nothing, I'm sure, that she wouldn't do."

When someone in the courtyard asked Peter if he'd been with Jesus, "Peter denied it, and at that moment a rooster began to crow" (John 18:26-27). Later, the angel told the women that Jesus had risen and to go tell the disciples. And Peter. Especially Peter (Mark 16:6-7). Jesus didn't say, "What he did was more than awful. I was the best friend that man will ever have. Well, it hurt too much. I cannot forgive it. I will not."

"He poured water into a basin and began to wash his disciples' feet, drying them with the towel that was wrapped around him" (John 13:5). He didn't say — "Let someone else do it; certainly it's not my place to wash someone's dirty feet."

God's Son never said any of those kinds of things. Instead He came and taught us to love and care for others and simply not worry about self.

Christians all over the world are learning the lesson. They are putting self aside and letting Christ live in them. These children of God try not to hurt others. Instead they help, showing Jesus they love Him by finding many ways to "feed His sheep."

One way is to keep on teaching so that brothers and sisters can grow in the Lord, when by all rights, someone else should take over. My mom taught a high school Sunday school class for twenty years. She was motivated by love for her students and her Lord. One year at Christmas there was a present under the tree from two boys who were once in her class and now in college. We open our presents "decently and in order" at Mother's house, so I happened to see her open the gift, gasp, and put her hands up to eyes that were filling with tears. The young men had searched for, bought, wrapped, and brought out to Mom a wooden plaque with a rose etched on it along with the simple words: "You have touched me — I have grown." Oh, that that could be said of me! Of all of us. Over and over again.

Another way is to help and encourage. My sister has a beauty shop and works long hours. Her arms and her back always hurt, yet I remember the times she has taken her day off to go to a Christian children's home to give haircuts to everyone who wanted one. She often finds time to do something nice to make people happy. Like beautifully cross-stitching a book mark for every lady who attended a banquet at her church. She worked on the book marks for several evenings when she came from work, and the last night, she sat in her rocker working so long that she heard birds chirping. Morning had come. She put the last book mark away and got ready for work.

Men can be as thoughtful. I remember a fellow in our church getting stranded when his car broke down five hundred miles away from home. Two of our men called him and told him not to worry, they'd be there the next day with a trailer to tow his car home and a car to bring his family home.

Some people take the time to write letters to or go see people who miss church. My dad wrote a young couple who had missed church five Sundays in a row. He quoted a statistic that said when people miss that many Sundays, they usually don't come back. He said he was writing because he loved them. They were in church the next Sunday.

Then there are those who help instead of hurt the "fallen." They need help so badly. I heard of a woman who committed adultery and could not stand the pain of what she'd done. Because she did not understand or believe the promise of forgiveness which is detailed so beautifully and thoroughly in God's word, she pulled down the garage door, sat in her car and turned on the ignition. That's how her family found her. But for many others, God's saints have come to the rescue, holding out the redemptive love of God. They fight a spiritual battle, pouring their lives into these brothers and sisters with a love that will not let go. Sometimes they lose, but often they win. They strive arduously, though the battle can go either way, because they know this is God's will: "My brothers, if one of you should wander from the truth and someone should bring him back, remember this: Whoever turns a sinner away from his error will save him from death and cover over a multitude of sins" (James 5:19-20).

There are those who wash feet and feed sheep by forgiving unfairness and abuse. They try to understand another's point of view. My daughter Leanne is married now, living and attending church in a little community forty-five miles from Joplin. She and her husband are very involved in the work there, and last year, even though she was in college and it was finals week, and even though she was only twenty years old, she was put in charge of the Christmas banquet. The lady responsible for the food worked with her husband in their store and could not leave to shop, so Leanne went by there to see if she could help. While they talked, the lady asked about decorations for the dinner. Leanne explained that she was thinking of something simple, like candles with greenery around the base. That's when the lady's husband came storming out of the back room. His wife had just mentioned that candles would make people sick in the poorly ventilated room. Now her husband informed Leanne that those in charge were apparently "Catholic sympathizers," and worse than that, they only wanted to use candles to ward off evil spirits. He ended his tirade by telling her that he would not be coming to the banquet.

During this verbal attack, Leanne had tried to reason with him. Finally she left, saying "I'm sorry you feel that way."

Later when she called and told me what happened, I was horrified. It was all I could do not to get in the car and go explain to that man how to talk to my "baby." But I controlled myself and stayed in my kitchen, talking sweetly to my child, trying to soothe away her hurt. When we were both better, I got a little crazy and told her all the things she could have said. For instance, when he said he wasn't coming, she could have said, "Wow, the candles are already working!"

Of course, I didn't really want Leanne to say that and was glad the worst she said was, "I'm sorry you feel that way." Before we hung up, she told me he was a good man in a lot of ways. And she assured me it would be fine.

I was proud of Leanne. I wondered if she remembered a bad day I had had several years earlier. She and I sat in my car in a friend's drive-

TRYING TO UNDERSTAND

way. My teenager held my hand while tears streamed down my face as I whispered a prayer (I could speak no louder, because of the pain in my throat). I prayed that God would help me reach out to a friend who had hurt me. In my own words I prayed St. Francis' prayer: I asked that I not desire to be understood or consoled but that in His name I would understand and console my friend. I remember how hard it was, how scared I was to do this most unnatural thing. And I remember how free I felt when God helped me do it.

I pray parts of an anonymous Christmas poem often. It asks us to come in silence to the manger, to behold our holiness made visible. It asks that we "lay before the newly born," nothing but our self-concern: our grasping, our sickly pride, our hidden venom, our little love. The opportunities to do so come almost daily.

The Son of God was willing to become a baby to warm us with His love and willing to kneel at the dirty feet of His disciples to show the extent of that love. When He finished, He asked, "Do you understand what I have done for you?"

And He waits for each of us to answer.

Chapter Eight

A Kind and Healthy Way

Because of my frame of reference, I have always felt "equal." Once when I was a teenager, Dad called my brother, sister and me into the kitchen to look at an assortment of partially-filled containers which he had arranged all over the counter. It was horrifying to see things that had once been edible covered with various shades of green and yellow mold. What was not molded was cracked and dried. From this smorgasbord Dad told us to decide what we wanted for dinner. My dad, with his sick sense of humor, was cleaning out the refrigerator and wanted to share the experience with us. He was a railroad engineer who kept all sorts of odd hours, and Mom was a private secretary. There were no boundaries drawn for what a woman should do and what a man should do. Each of them did what had to be done, when it had to be done. (The refrigerator, apparently, had been a stand-off.)

I married a man who is also not much interested in "roles." Tony and I are very different; the most casual observer could see that. He has more self-discipline in some areas than I. He will cheerfully and enthusiastically get up at 4:00 a.m. to get an early start on some destination or to go hunting. I, on the other hand, never rise cheerfully and feel to do so before 7:00 is primitive.

Tony also has more strength and energy. He can work eight hours, grab a quick bite to eat, paint the house from 6 to 9, do the church financial statement from 9 until 11, and finally turn out the light and go to sleep as though he has done nothing. All of this he does without groaning – "I AM SO TIRED!" I start that refrain right after lunch. Somehow, saying that always makes me feel better.

Too, Tony is more practical. What he said one morning is typical. While sitting at my vanity applying make-up, I paused, pensively, with mascara brush in mid-air, and sighed, "Tony, how very quickly we get to be middle-aged."

He was sitting on the fireplace hearth tying his shoes. He sounded half disgusted with my peculiar point-of-view when he glanced over at me and said, "Quickly! It took 40 years!"

Yet as different as we are, Tony has never said,

and I'm sure never even thought, we were unequal. He encouraged me to go back to school, because he thought I would be a good teacher. And when I did go back, he helped me. Taking care of our children was his privilege as well as mine. We have developed a lifestyle that suits us – our interests, our talents, our schedules. Life is a mutual thing with very few lines drawn. It is a kind and healthy way.

I'm sure this kind of background influences my thinking. I hope it does not influence or distort my reading of the scripture. For when I read the Bible, I always see God using women in leadership roles just as He used men. Miriam helped lead the people out of Israel (Exod. 15:20). Deborah, along with Barak, was a judge of Israel, a spiritual leader as well as a civil and military leader (Judges 4:5). Huldah (II Kings 22:12-20) and Isaiah's wife (Isaiah 8:1-4) in the Old Testament and Phillip's four daughters in the New Testament (Acts 21:9) were prophetesses. Phoebe (Romans 16:2) was a deaconess, and Paul told the people to help her with whatever she needed. Priscilla helped her husband Aquila teach the mighty preacher, Apollos. These accounts and many others make me feel that God, even in a culture that considered women more "things" than people, let women lead.

Still, although God used women in many ways, that was not the norm. In Jesus' day and before, women, both Jew and Gentile, had few options. I'm glad I was not born there and then.

I'm also glad I didn't live in sixteenth century

Scotland. Patricia Gundry in her essay, "Why We're Here," tells the story of Eufame MacLayne. She was pregnant with twins, carrying them in an odd position which caused her a long and difficult labor. After much suffering, she requested a painkilling herb and finally delivered two healthy babies. That all three lived was miraculous. Unfortunately, however, in that day painkillers were forbidden in childbirth because the Bible "clearly states" that women are supposed to suffer in childbirth, as punishment for Eve's sin. Consequently, the leaders judged Eufame, found her guilty, and took her babies from her arms and gave them to someone else. Then they burned her alive (*Women, Authority and the Bible, 12-13*).

People who have read the Bible with a strict "black or white" mentality have done horrible things throughout history – sometimes changing lives from what they might have been, sometimes even taking lives. Yet their firm stand and enforcement of what they considered to be biblical teaching may have given no consideration for context (they say you can make the Bible say almost anything), word meanings, historical and cultural background, or other scriptures. That could be true in late 20th century America also, so dialogue about woman's place in the church today is important. Cultural background alone gives us much to consider.

Our culture is not the culture of Paul's day, where the testimony of women was not accepted. Walter Liefeld suggests that Paul may not have specifically mentioned that the women were the first to the tomb when he cited witnesses of the resurrection because of that lack of acceptance *(Women, Authority and the Bible, 223)*.

Now, not only is woman's testimony accepted, but she often "judges" testimony. We do not think it extraordinary to find a woman judge in today's courtroom. In our day women are doctors, lawyers, astronauts and executives. Our age is not Shakespeare's stage where males had to play both men's and women's roles because women were not allowed to perform on stage.

Strange it took so long. For change for all the world became a possibility with Jesus. He showed us what God thinks when He did what no other man in His day would have done – He spoke openly and respectfully to the woman at the well. Her response was to leave her waterpot to go tell the men in her town that she had found Christ (John 4:6-30). There must be layer after layer of meaning in that brief encounter. But one thing is sure: in that moment, Jesus crushed the barriers of race, class, sex and sin. In that instant, the common prayer of the male Jew – "Thank you, God that I am not a Gentile, a slave, or a woman" – began its evolution from no-longer-applicable to ludicrous.

Women have always celebrated and given thanks for what Jesus has done for them. But today we can serve and tell of our redemption in much the same way men have always been able to. That opportunity makes sense of the fact that women were the first to hear and know the Good News. And the first to tell it. I'm so glad to be living now when woman's opportunity to respond is so great.

However, although we women are free to do many things, that does not take away the fact that we've been asked to be submissive to elders (or a husband, in the case of the home). This might be easier to accept if we understand that subordination, no matter how abhorrent the word in modern America, does not mean inferiority or anything else negative. There is a necessary order needed if any organization, large like a church or small like a home, is to survive and thrive. Nearly all of us have willingly placed ourselves in many submissive roles in one way or another. Those roles are everywhere.

The idea of submission is also easier to accept when we remember that God's men and women both are subject to one another, or so it says in Ephesians 5:21. That verse could be considered the thesis of the "wives and husbands" section of Ephesians 5. Submission is at the heart of Christianity. Christ Himself who "did not consider equality with God something to be grasped" is the example for us all (Phil. 2:6).

Even when I get that straight, I still struggle with the two tiny, but incredibly major passages, I Corinthians 14:34 and I Timothy 2:11-15. (They are major, given the material written about them and the decisions based on them). I imagine there are a lot of women out there who understand how

I feel. I read one explanation of these controversial passages and think it sound. Then honest and searching, I read an opposite interpretation and find it sound and convincing as well. I hope James did not have the woman's issue in mind when he cautioned us not to be doubters, who are "blown and tossed by the wind" (1:6), because I just do not know what is right – not with certainty.

So I do what I always do, even in the middle of such controversy and confusion, I try to get on with loving and serving God and His people. I take my non-revolutionary spirit and do whatever anyone asks me to do or will let me do (that I *can* do, of course). And if someone does not want me to do something for whatever reason, that is fine with me, I have plenty to do otherwise.

Generally speaking, my feelings are not easily hurt. So as an English teacher at a conservative Bible college, when I have had a male student who would not take my courses or attend a "lecture" I was giving because I'm a woman (and it happens seldom), I have not worried much about it. I never say anything. But in my heart I feel sad for these male students (and to some extent, for the people to whom they will minister), because they choose not to hear a feminine perspective and are, therefore, diminished. I've also felt, instinctively, and possibly wrongly, that they were ignorant.

But wherever we stand on this issue as we continue the struggle for truth, we must never forget that the basic and necessary element in our Christian lives is love. That must affect our actions and our attitudes.

After I had been married many years, I saw a man I had dated in college. He was thrilled by my ministry of teaching, writing, and speaking. He mentioned, however, that if I had married *him*, he imagined he wouldn't have let me go back to school to get my degrees. It was just a casual comment, but I've thought about it since. What if *anyone* had kept me from developing my strong points? What a waste that seems. How unloving. It seems so wrong. Even unscriptural, if it, in fact, does violate the law of love. Why would anyone keep anyone else from doing what he/she can do best, if it does not in any way shame the gospel?

And our attitudes should be as loving as our actions. Many years ago the elders of the church I grew up in asked my mom, a long-time teacher of the senior high class, to teach the Young Married's class for several weeks. The first Sunday morning, well-prepared and cheerfully excited, she began class. After she was well under way, a young man raised his hand and stated loudly and firmly that he, a man, refused to be taught by a woman. Mom, rather put-on-the-spot, immediately turned the class into a discussion format, with no one "teaching." I've always felt the man in that particular situation, a clod, and my mom, very gracious. One attitude was unloving, the other, loving.

Both sexes are capable of unloving attitudes. We Christian women cannot be so frustrated or angry or impatient that we sound like the lady who substituted for a reporter on a network news magazine program. Since it was December, one segment of the program was a preview of a Charlie Brown Christmas special. It featured Linus, standing on a grade school stage, reciting the Bethlehem Story. His light little voice closed the touching excerpt with, "And peace on earth, good will to all men." As the camera returned to the newswoman, good will was blown to bits as she sneered, "And women and children and dogs and cats. . . ." More ignorance.

Maybe *she* can talk that way, but surely we cannot. *Always*, one thing is simple and clear: if men and women are Christians, in all cultures and for all time, they love.

Meanwhile, even among our very conservative churches, we now have women Christian Education Directors. One of these ladies was asked to speak at a sister congregation several years ago. When she got up to the pulpit to give her "speech," the man presiding, sitting behind her, coughed. She proceeded. He coughed again, a little more obviously. Finally, he got her attention so that he could let her know that she was to give her speech from behind the lectern which was beside the *pulpit*, not from behind the pulpit itself.

I'm sorry, but most people, wherever they are on this issue at the moment, will smile at that, at least a little. As for me, I couldn't help but laugh.

Oh well, it doesn't change the fact that she did speak. She got to tell the Good News, and male and female hearts were blessed.

Our Scottish sister, Eufame MacLayne, would

probably be amazed. She might think it a kind and healthy way.

Chapter Nine

The Reason the Rabbit Could Fly

I have never found life to be easy. I often feel like Woodstock, who has just crawled out of a cracked egg and has run into Snoopy. Snoopy kindly explains to his innocent bird friend that "our kind" have very little to say about how the world turns. With that truth, Woodstock turns around slump-shouldered and walks away. In the last frame of the cartoon, he is inside the egg pulling the top back down over himself with a sigh. No confidence.

There have been enough times I've wanted to curl up in the fetal position and pull the top of the egg down over me. I certainly thought about it the September of my 30th year. That's when I started teaching.

It only took one week for me to realize that I wasn't going to make it.

Once I had made up my mind to return to school and had done well in a few classes, I had assumed, poor naive woman, that I would be a good teacher. My assumptions were crushed during this first week. My problems had nothing to do with liking the high school students or with maintaining discipline. Both were easy for me. In fact, it took me some time to figure out exactly what my problem was. When I did, I realized I had never heard of it before. One hundred and fifty hours of college — and I had never heard of it.

In its simplest form, I did not know how to transfer what I knew to my students: I could recognize and punctuate a complex sentence, but wasn't sure how to get my students to do the same. I knew a good short story when I read one, but did not know how to bring my students to that point. My one probing question when we finished "The Most Dangerous Game" was "Well, now, wasn't that interesting?"

This was a terrifying realization when I had six classes to face each day. One hundred and fifty kids (coincidentally, one for every college hour I had completed) were counting on me.

Tony was never sweeter. He came into our bedroom one evening during the second week and found me curled up on the bed, clutching one of my books and staring at the flowers on the wallpaper. He sat down on the bed and looked at me.

Then he slid my book out of my hands and leafed through it, suggesting different things I might be able to try next. "Let me quit," I mumbled.

I'm sure he was tempted. He had seen things in the last week that unnerved even him a bit. When we went somewhere together in the car, I sat there saying absolutely nothing. Nothing. I couldn't talk.

I couldn't eat either. Or sleep. I think what happened one day in class, the last straw, I suppose, was related to not sleeping for so long. I was standing before my third hour class when someone said something funny. A tiny remnant of my sense-of-humor was still hanging on, and I smiled. The students smiled. Then, when it was appropriate, the students stopped smiling. Ninth graders, but totally socialized. I, on the other hand, did not stop smiling. Not that I didn't want to. But I couldn't. I guess my involuntary muscles shut down. Even the voluntary ones, because when I *told* myself to quit smiling, I still didn't. I finally turned around and pushed my smile down. Then, thank God, the bell rang.

I guess it was right after that incident that I marched down to the office and told them to get a substitute for me the next day, because I planned on being sick.

The next morning I walked into the unemployment office to become a secretary or something. They looked at me like I hadn't slept in a week, and I left. On my way home, I stopped by the college where I had attended and saw some of my old professors. They told me, in short, that I wanted to teach like they do, except they'd been teaching for twenty years, not one week. And they told me if I quit, they never wanted to see me again.

Several other things happened that weekend to encourage me to stick it out. I went back that next Monday with Tony's promise ringing in my ears: "Just teach till Christmas; then you can quit." Till Christmas, I thought. Tony was playing an old game: he knew if I made it until Christmas, I'd make it period.

And sure enough, by sometime in October I was perfectly ok (as ok as I ever am). I loved teaching, just as I knew I would, and I slowly but surely learned how to get all that information across. Although that was fifteen years ago, I'll never forget it, because it was one of my most terrifying experiences. Such utter lack of confidence. Such gripping fear.

Of course, that wouldn't have happened to me if I hadn't stepped into a new experience. But life is stepping into new experiences and placing ourselves where we aren't always emotionally and physically safe. If we aren't willing to take risks, I'm not sure that we aren't guilty of burying our talent. The one-talent man was afraid; he lacked confidence, hid his talent, played it safe, and he was cast into darkness (Matt. 25).

So hopefully we will choose to "step out," grow, expand, venture. But facing the unknown almost always produces fear. When we realize, however, that we are not alone, that God is with us supplying all we will need for any situation, we will no longer have a "spirit of timidity." Glimpsing what God is willing to do in us gives us confidence. It might look as if we have self-confidence, but actually we have God-confidence. And there is nothing like living, God confident.

Still we sometimes buy into the popular philosophy that we can do it ourselves. At some point, though, most of us come to the end of self-confidence, and our world crumbles around us. There is an obvious biblical example of this. Samson at one time knew his source of strength was God, but he forgot it and began relying on himself. Samson's self-confidence and pride only produced blindness, captivity, and mockery. Grinding in the prison, bound in shackles and with his eyes gouged out, he was not living the life God had intended.

It might seem ironic to those who don't understand what God can do, that Samson, now weak, broken and empty, was ready for his greatest moment. He remembered his source and called upon his God, in whom he could be confident, and destroyed the house of the false god of the Philistines (Judges 16:28).

Too often we're like Samson, relying totally on ourselves to do things, or assessing only ourselves before we try to do anything. God wants us to know that He is our source of strength, and always we should factor that in.

That's why He had Gideon send away 31,700 of the men he had gathered to fight the Midianites, keeping only 300. He will work with us. He does not send us out alone. He took the three hundred and beat an army whose "camels could no more be counted than the sand on the seashore" (Judges 7).

God can do unthinkable things in us — if we could believe Him. David, Joshua and Caleb did the improbable and impossible because of the confidence they had in their God.

Even as a child David took on the Philistine giant when all the other men of Israel were too afraid to try. David reassures Saul and boldly states his faith in God: "The Lord who delivered me from the paw of the lion and the paw of the bear, will deliver me from the hand of this Philistine" (I Sam. 17:37).

Joshua and Caleb believed the promised land could be taken. What was the difference between these two spies and the other ten? The ten did not factor in God when they saw the challenge before them, so they certainly didn't seek this new experience. Joshua and Caleb, on the other hand, were confident that God would go before them. In fact, they had only one fear — the fear of not allowing God to work through them:

> Only do not rebel against the Lord. And do not be afraid of the people of the land, because we will swallow them up. Their protection is gone, but the Lord is with us. Do not be afraid of them (Numbers 14:8-9).

As it has often been pointed out, God's purposes will always be accomplished, ultimately, but will

THE REASON THE RABBIT COULD FLY

we be a part of it? These fearful people were not part of this particular victory. Except for Joshua and Caleb, those who believed in the power of "God in us."

The only difference in these men and other men and women of Israel is their "real" confidence in a living God. The others were still God's children, but how different their lives were, how different their experience with God.

Paul tapped into God's power, too. "I can do everything through him who gives me strength" (Phil. 4:13). Too often we profane his resolve. In fairness, I suppose we believe it intellectually, but it seems like we say it with the same kind of gusto Paul did, until something challenging comes along. Then some don't say it at all. Maybe we haven't come to believe it like Paul, because we've not tested the truth of it enough. Paul surely had. He had been flogged with 39 stripes five times, he had been beaten three times, he had been stoned, shipwrecked three times, he had been cold and hungry, in one peril after another (II Cor. 11); yet he pressed on, to any new experience God might have for him, confident that God would continue to make him able.

I don't expect to fight a bear, lion, or giant. I don't expect to fight the Philistines, or to face the perils Paul faced. But I do expect to grow and experience new and exciting things in my world for and with the Lord. I hope I have finally learned to say, "I know whom I have believed" (II Tim. 1:12), and I know He takes my weakness and makes me strong (Heb. 1:34).

Paul prays we will come to know the "incomparably great power" God has for those who believe. A power "like the working of his mighty strength, which he exerted in Christ when he raised him from the dead and seated him at his right hand in the heavenly realms" (Eph. 1:19-20). If you believe, what kind of things will happen, because He exerts His mighty strength in you?

She didn't believe she could witness to her non-Christian neighbors, but she trusted Eph. 1:20, and she did.

They both suffered from extreme stuttering, a speech impediment which made public speaking virtually impossible. However, they also both believed in that power which God "exerted in Christ when he raised him from the dead." They've both been preaching the gospel effectively for over thirty years.

She had been smoking for thirty years and had always wanted not to. When she made her decision to quit, a doctor told her a wonderful method that causes people to quit smoking in as few as six weeks. She appreciated the doctor's concern, but she knew she had a "Savior who could do it in one day."

She was terrified to stand before a group of people and lead songs, but she loved people, and she loved music, and after preparing herself in every way possible, she took her shaking knees, her fluttering heart, and God's promise of power and stood before the congregation to begin her songleading ministry.

Her friend hurt her, but then she had hurt her friend, too. It seemed they would never be able to make it right. She decided to try to restore their friendship, but fear and pride had a tight grip. She asked for the power of God's Spirit to enable her to reach out. It seemed impossible, but Eph. 1:20 let her dare.

She was only 52 when he died. Her children were grown. All her life revolved around him; why, she couldn't even drive. She loved him so. What would she do? How could she do it? Power enabled her to learn to drive, to buy a car, to take care of bills when she had never done so before. Power enabled her to build a life alone — one that is productive and satisfying.

Their mother was a tremendous force in the lives of these two brothers who became Christian leaders. When she learned she was terminally ill, she told her sons that she had taught them how to live and now she would teach them how to die. She lived every moment of her life by the power which raised Christ from the dead.

When Jesus raised Lazarus from the dead, He came to the tomb, which was a "cave with a stone laid across the entrance" (John 11:38), and asked that they "Take away the stone." What He asked should get our attention, because Jesus did not need for them to do that. If He could raise Lazarus, He could move a stone while he was at it. A songwriter has suggested that their participation was symbolic of what we must do if the power of God is to work in our lives: roll back the stone of doubt in our hearts. I try to remember that Jesus did not do many "mighty works" or "miracles" in His home town "because of their lack of faith" (Matthew 13:58).

We're all kind of like this crazy bird I once heard about. He thought he was a rabbit. I can't recall why, but I do know he grew up with rabbits, ate rabbit food, played rabbit games, and got around by hopping. One day a certain owl mentioned to this bird that he wasn't really a rabbit at all, but that he was bird. The bird was outraged by such a suggestion and snipped, "Of course, I'm a rabbit." (He believed the flaps on his sides were a deformity.) He was a rabbit!

One day the bird was hopping around on a high cliff. Unfortunately, the owl was, too, and he pushed the bird right off the edge, hollering, "You're a bird, and if I were you, I'd flap those wings. You'll see you can fly."

Because this suggestion beat anything else the bird could think of as he torpedoed toward the ground, the bird who insisted he was a rabbit flapped his wings and began to soar through the air — a bird.

The point is, we are more than we think we are, too. We are not completely human, not us. We, too, can soar, for we are empowered by God Himself; we are "partakers of the divine nature" (II Peter 1:4), and in us He will do "immeasurably more than all we ask or imagine, according to His power that is at work within us" (Eph. 3:20).

Chapter Ten

Peace in the Middle of the Mess

I like to receive letters from my brother Roger (alias Bog; Gerson Smoger; Tyrone Goodenplenty; and the latest, Clay Mayshun — I never know how he'll sign his letters). I like to write him, too. That has nothing to do with how much I love him. I love lots of people I seldom write. It has to do with the fact that he stretches me. He appreciates reading the comical, the bizarre, or the deep. Anything but the ordinary. I try never to begin with (or even include) a report on weather conditions or a description of my new shoes.

To an extent, this has spilled over into my other personal letters. I wrote a letter to a friend last spring and made a confession of sorts. This, alone, can make a letter uncommon. Friends, I have noticed, enjoy "revelation." I probably could have divulged something more arresting; nevertheless, I wrote a fact about myself significant enough that I recall writing it: "This is a busy, as in hectic, time for me. I wish I could be more organized and avoid any feeling of the frantic. I would like to be serene."

There you have it, one of my deepest wishes — I would like to be serene.

Not that I haven't experienced serenity. But I wrote that letter in April, and I seldom experience serenity then. In April there are thousands of papers to grade and it seems like that many lectures to give in the classroom and behind various lecterns around the country. So about the time the flowers bloom each spring, I take a poster off my bulletin board in my office and tack it up on the one in my classroom. It is a pencil drawing of a woman, from the shoulders up. She is harried, rather emaciated looking. What hair she has is sticking straight out all over her head, and her eyes are wide and glazed. Her appearance makes the caption underneath her portrait believable: "I had one nerve left when I got up this morning, and you're on it." My students laugh.

Yet the same students that laugh at this pencil portrait know what my funeral song is. I hope they more often think of me when they hear the lyrics of that song, rather than when they think of that poster. I tell them that the song is what I aspire to, that I will have lived the truth of it by the time God calls me home. I want to know God so well and trust Him so completely that I can truly say, "It is well with my soul."

I think it is possible for peace to fill us even in the busy Aprils of our lives. I believe we can have peace even when circumstances worse than a hectic schedule frustrate us.

"Frustrated" is how my friend described the despair she felt when she moved across the country to a small town, for she had left a spirit-filled congregation and become part of a very apathetic one. There were few young couples, and the ones that were there attended only Sunday school, leaving before the worship service. She felt her needs could never be met in that kind of environment. "Sorrows like sea billows" were rolling.

Being frustrated is miserable. The helplessness and hopelessness often associated with it are crippling. All of us face such frustrations, and a study of the first chapter of Philippians has helped me deal with my own.

Several reasons for Paul to be frustrated are recorded in this chapter: he misses those he loves (vv. 7-8), he is in jail (vv. 12-14), he is aware that some preach the Gospel with impure motives (vv. 15, 17), and he knows there are those who are against him (v. 17). Yet, Paul, with a variety of problems, seems peaceful. He implicitly, if not explicitly, encourages the Philippians, and us, to be at least four things. If we can, we can reduce, and maybe even eliminate, frustration. We can find peace in the middle of the mess.

BE REALISTIC

I daydream sometimes. I thought I was the champion until I read a column the other day, Joyce Brothers' I think, that said all of us daydream between 30 and 40 per cent of our waking hours. I don't know if that's good or bad; she seemed to think it was good. Like a lot of things, I guess it has the potential to be either. We keep ourselves from being bored when engaged in mindless tasks, we make plans, we escape. One of the first daydreams I remember having was formulated on the grade school playground. In my mind, I pretended my name was Pat. A variation of it was pretending my name was Pam. Short and easy to say. Escape. This bashful little girl did not want to experience one more tall, imposing teacher standing over me with a puzzled look on her face saying, "Ja what?"

Jackina rhymes with China, or better yet, Shekinah. It does not rhyme with Treena, Lena, or Regina. But how would anyone know that? Even today, I consider putting a straight line over the *I*, making it a long vowel sound. So maybe you can understand — the little girl daydreamed. (In my old age I've given up the silly daydream of having the name Pat or Pam. I now prefer Hannah or Claire.)

So who am I to write about realism? Strangely enough, I am a fairly realistic daydreamer. Even though I have occasionally been transformed into a Pat, soaking up the April sun on the beach outside my condominium on Myrtle Beach, I do see myself and my world fairly clearly. For instance, I can call a spade a spade. I don't allow myself excuses. I get rid of rationalizations pretty quickly and deal with what is.

I doubt Paul daydreamed (his name is easy), but whether he did or not, he was a master realist. He was certainly realistic about his imprisonment: he knows that what has happened to him "has *really* served to advance the gospel" (v. 12) (emphasis mine). Paul saw his situation clearly. He stepped back, mentally, and understood that good things were happening as a result of his imprisonment and this, perhaps, reduced his frustration. Besides that, he understood that he could do very little to alter the situation anyway. And then, too, one of the great bottom lines of the Christian life, whether he lived or died, he would live in and for Christ, and this reality, his strong purpose, probably alleviated frustration as much as anything (vv. 20-21).

When we were going together, my husband gave me a charm bracelet with a little prayer on it which you may have seen (not on my bracelet, however, because I lost it). It goes something like this:

> Lord, grant me the courage to change the things I can change, the serenity to accept what I can *not* change, and the wisdom to know the difference.

Paul had this ability. What is frustrating you? Be

realistic. Is it something you can do something about? *Really*? If so, systematically set about to do just that. Don't waste another frustrating minute: get you a plan and act on it. Or is what is frustrating you something you can do absolutely nothing about? Then you need to lay it down. Give it to God, learn from it. Do whatever is appropriate, but no longer struggle with it. Have the grace to accept it.

I have been frustrated from time to time by the way I've handled certain situations with my brothers and sisters in Christ. I am very sensitive to that and take seriously the admonitions to go to my brother when there is a problem. I've learned that division occurs when we do not and also, that God's spirit is hampered (within us and within the church).

Scripture tells us that "if it is possible, as far as it depends on you, live at peace with everyone" (Rom. 12:18). It also tells us to make "every effort" to live in peace (Heb. 12:14). So, remembering the Hebrews passage, I've gone fairly often, and the communicating has helped. But we may face a moment when a part of the Romans passage, "as far as it depends on you," is also applicable. For various reasons, peace is deferred. We can't make things "right," or at least like we would like them to be. So, realistically, when we've done all we can do, we must accept the situation (never forgetting to continue praying). We shouldn't drive ourselves crazy and waste precious energy that could be put to good use somewhere else.

BE POSITIVE

I like to think I'm a positive person, yet something happened when I first started writing that made me reassess. I was not in a very good mood as I sort of stalked out to the mailbox. When I reached in to pull out several envelopes, a thick letter from a familiar publishing company was on top. Out loud, mind you, I said, "Oh great, yet another one!" Meaning a rejection. Fat envelopes are always bad news; it's your manuscript, plus the nice form rejection letter. So I stuck it on bottom and took the bunch into the house and sat down in the corduroy recliner to look over the bills leisurely, dreading looking at the anticipated rejection. One bill I happened to look at was $63 for the repair of my typewriter. I was in no mood for irony. I looked at it negatively (and out loud again) snipped, "I'd like to know what I need a typewriter for anyway." I was sort of kidding, but serious enough that I was a little ashamed when I opened the letter and found out the article had been accepted. (It was fat, in fact, because two articles had been accepted, and they had returned my extra envelope.)

Most of the time, I really am positive. I know positive helps and negative never does. Not long before Leanne started sixth grade, we passed her school, and she announced to me as she glanced over at it, that she believed she was going to have a "successful" school year. Sure enough, her grades went from a-little-above-average to straight

A's. When we were going somewhere in the car a few days after her report card came out, I played the roving reporter and asked her how this came to be. She looked at my thumb/microphone. Then, after some thought, she leaned into the mike and proudly and emphatically declared, "Work, Work, Work!"

While that may be true, I do believe her positive attitude made the real difference. She walked through those double doors in September to bring home A's.

A positive point of view fights frustration. It is maybe half of what is needed to cope. It makes a remarkable difference. Paul wasn't negative about his chains because with them he could tell a captive audience of palace guards about Christ. In addition, many Christians were courageously speaking the word since Paul was restricted (vv. 13-14). Think of it, this may have been the first intern program. Under the best of circumstances, Paul would not be there forever to preach, and he could encourage and teach those who were "forced" to take over for him.

He continues to be positive when discussing the people who were insincerely preaching the gospel out of "envy and rivalry" and "selfish ambition" in order to stir up trouble for him. For me, this is the apex of positive: "But what does it matter?" he asks. "The important thing is that in every way, whether from false motives or true, Christ is preached." Now that's positive.

BE THANKFUL

Mother bent over my bed just before they took me to the delivery room to give birth to my first baby, her first grandbaby. She wanted to tell me something. She kissed my forehead and said, "You are taking the pain of this date away from me." Until that moment, I didn't know my mom had lost her first baby on November 23, the day Stacey was born.

Mother has a thankful spirit. She's had heartache in her life, but she always tells me not to worry about it because God has given her so much joy. The heartache does not matter.

I seldom see her thankfulness waver. But one Thanksgiving it did. She calls it Black Thursday. Her dinner was behind schedule, her disposition was regressing, as she herself put it, from "its usual bad to horrid," and she was taking her frustration out on the onion and green pepper in a hand-held food chopper. Unfortunately, the lid was not screwed down tightly, and slivers of onion and pepper flew all over the kitchen. I cleaned up the mess for Mom, but I could see that she was still quite unhappy.

She wasn't any happier ten minutes later, when the second disaster occurred. Checking the turkey for doneness, she managed to tip the oven rack, and "that miserable bird" wound up on the floor. Mother, losing her thankfulness but remaining realistic, picked her up, wiped her off and slammed her back into the oven.

Overwhelmed by that time with self-pity, she dragged out a leaf for the table, and refusing all offers of help, tugged and shoved and heaved and finally got the section in place. Then she slammed the table together, managing to catch the palm of her hand in the juncture, raising a monstrous blood blister.

Bless her heart. Even on Thanksgiving, it's sometimes hard to maintain a thankful spirit. (Eventually dinner was served, the debris was cleared away and serenity of a sort was restored. She even recovered sufficiently to tell me that someday — say year 2000 — she would laugh about it.)

God's Word says, fantastically enough, to *always* give thanks (Eph. 5:20). Do you mean even on Black Thursday when the the turkey falls on the floor?

Always, because it is true — "in all things God works for the good of those who love him" (Rom. 8:28). That is not to say all things are good. But for those of us who love and trust Him, those of us who will wait and will let Him, God will make even bad things good. We have often ended up calling bad things "blessings."

I used to have the hardest time understanding the word "blessings." I have a friend who feels he is very "blessed," and so he is, according to how we ordinarily use the word: he's healthy and handsome, and he has a beautiful family, a wonderful home, and a perfect job. I told him once that it was difficult for me to call those things blessings, because if he lost his job, someone in his family became ill, and all his possessions were destroyed in a fire, would I then have to say he was *not* blessed? Are so many of God's people with so much pain *not* blessed?

One day I finally realized something very basic — yes, if they're God's children, they *are* blessed. God is in control, and he cares for all his children. Therefore, while health, possessions, a good job are blessings, illness, losing our worldly possessions, or losing a valued job can also turn into blessings. God is working in all and through all, and He, whatever the circumstances, is blessing.

I love and admire Tony's mother for many reasons. One is this very thing I'm talking about. She has had half of her stomach removed because of cancer, she has lost her husband and sisters, and she struggles every day of her life just to breathe. But she doesn't talk about what she has lost or what she cannot do; she talks about what she has and what she *can* do. I believe she trusts God and truly believes He can turn what seems bad into good. She always gives thanks and beats the frustrations that often accompany difficulties.

I hope I'm learning this lesson, even though I have yet to face what my mother-in-law has. One evening at the close of what was for me a miserable writing conference, I sat alone in my room and wrote in my prayer journal a list of the painful things I had learned that week. At the close of my four-page entry, I wrote these two sentences:

I hated these days, Lord.
Thank you for them.

I meant it.

Paul begins his letter with thanks, and that thankful spirit is evident throughout the whole first chapter as he rejoices because the gospel is preached (v. 18) and because he knows, one way or another, he will be delivered (v. 19).

BE TOUGH
(or determine to do the difficult)

Besides being realistic, positive and thankful, Paul was just plain tough and encouraged us to be. With the spirit of "I can do everything through him who gives me strength" (Phil. 4: 13), determine to do the difficult. Sometimes that means knowing what is right or good or needed and simply doing it. And if doing it threatens self-gratification, that *is* difficult in a society which sells the magazine SELF at checkout counters.

But if doing the right or good or needed is difficult, it is, also, always worth it. You make a good trade. The principle works in both simple and complex situations.

I mentioned that periodically I recommit myself to physical fitness. I had to do that this summer. By the end of the school year, I had had it on almost every level, especially physically.

I dragged myself over to the fitness center for a

fitness test. I knew I was not going to do well, but I was horrified when my upper and lower body strength measured on the fourth of four levels in the POOR category. If this were to change, I would have to be tough and do the "needed." So all summer long, I put on my headphones and listened to Steve Camp's "Doing My Best" tape while I walked three to six miles every day. With the same regularity, I did floor exercises to Annie Herring's "Waiting for My Ride to Come." Then three times a week, without tape accompaniment, I worked out on the weight machines.

I worked hard. I remember after four weeks, measuring and weighing and discovering I had not lost 1/4 of an inch or 1/2 pound. What I did at that point is very unlike me. I ignored those two discouraging facts and kept going, believing eventually it would pay off. Five months later, I had lost ten pounds and eight inches. More importantly, I felt strong again.

But I paid a price. I wonder if you could know how tough it is for me to get up at six in the summer. I also hate sweating and aching. But the results of becoming fit are simply worth it.

Commitment is tough in more general and serious ways, too. We tend to make the seemingly easier choice. For many, in certain phases of their less-than-satisfying (stimulating, exciting, fulfilling) marriages, the easier answer is divorce. In still other situations, for everyone's sake, we should leave, but that choice is too difficult, and we perpetuate abuse. The concept of tough love confronts that weakness.

For many, when difficult problems arise in our local churches, the easiest answers are to overlook it, leaving the problem to grow and fester, or to aimlessly "discuss" it with people unable to do anything about it, or to give up altogether and leave. We need to be tough and face problems. Finding the right, good, or needed answer is better and more satisfying.

Determining to do the difficult is basic to the Christian life. Paul is tough and encourages others to be: "Whatever happens, conduct yourselves in a manner worthy of the gospel of Christ" (vv. 27-28). He went on to say that if they did, he knew they would stand firm in the faith without fear of any who would oppose them. It might be difficult to walk worthy of the gospel, but if we do, we will also stand courageously firm in the faith.

When we are tough, we, with God's help, can reduce not only the frustration of a present situation, but we can also, in many cases, keep other frustrating circumstances from occurring. Be tough, using all your inner strength to do whatever needs to be done.

I saw my friend not long ago, the one who was so frustrated about the church situation she was in. I spoke at that church for a Ladies Day and ate lunch with her. She was beaming: things were very "well" with her soul. I had noticed that the church was packed for the service upstairs, but that was only the beginning of the good things that had happened there. In only four or five years, there had been a complete reversal. They had recently gone to two Sunday morning worship services, and they had just bought several scenic acres just outside of town to build a new church.

I remembered the letter I had written to her when she had been so upset years earlier. I had wanted to comfort her. I ended up talking about these principles from the first chapter of Philippians. These four things are the only things I know to do or be when we face such frustration.

In the end, being realistic, positive, thankful, and tough may bring me to the spiritual maturity I desire so much. Then the song just might sum up my life after all — no matter what, it was "well with my soul."

Chapter Eleven

I Call Him Joy

Tucking the girls in one night, I tried to hold back my mounting hysteria — at least until they were asleep. As soon as they closed their little eyes and were breathing deeply and evenly, I let go and threw myself across my bed and cried, off and on, for several hours. If only it were this morning, I lamented, and I still had my wedding ring.

It wasn't the *first* wedding ring I had lost. It was the second in ten years. The nightmare began that morning in the restroom at school. Not wanting to get handcream all over my ring, I took it off and put it on the chrome ledge over the sinks — two safe inches from my eyes. Then, through the swinging door came a girl I hadn't seen in years.

We talked and talked and somehow walked right out the door together and down the hall. I remembered my ring almost immediately and ran back to get it, but in the three minutes I had been gone, it had disappeared. My heart sank.

And now hours later, I sobbed. Tony wasn't home. He was still teaching and coaching at the time and out of town for a ballgame. In between crying spells, I tried to figure out how I would tell him about my second wedding ring, that neverending circle, symbol of our unending love. In between crying spells and speech organizing, I psychoanalyzed myself, thinking that losing my ring was possibly an outward manifestation of something deep and dire and that a sad sort of symbolism lay underneath it all. I was very unhappy.

When Tony came in about midnight, he assumed I was sleeping, turned on the television and flopped on the couch to unwind. The next thing he knew, I was flinging myself toward him in wild despair, landing on the floor by the couch and burying my head in his chest.

He asked if something were wrong.

After I had finally wailed everything out, he spoke as he always does: calmly and wisely. What he said had nothing to do with symbolism or manifestations. He simply said, "Well, what do you expect, Slick, you lose everything."

That's right! I thought. I do. Didn't my own father say he was taking me to the psychiatrist if I ever lost my purse again? And I'd lost it at least fifty times since then. Tony always makes me feel better. Soon I would be happy again.

That's the point, happiness comes and goes fairly quickly.

It has the same root word as happening, and it is dependent on circumstances. Joy, on the other hand, does not have to vacillate. I might have been pretty unhappy the night I lay sobbing across my bed mourning for my ring, but a close examination of my heart would have revealed that my joy was not gone. Unlike happiness, joy co-exists with sorrow. That's why Paul's letter to the Philippians can be filled with difficult circumstances and still mention joy nineteen times.

In John 16 Jesus tells his disciples two things that define joy for me: joy is the presence and provision of God.

THE PRESENCE OF GOD

Jesus had just told His disciples that soon they would see Him "no more." Before long, though, His miracle return would change the grief they would experience into joy, a joy, He said, that no one would take away (John 16:22). The source of this neverending joy is His presence.

God's presence being joy is a major theme throughout the word of God. King David is a picture of joy unleashed as he dances and celebrates "before the Lord with all his might" when the ark of the Lord is returned to Jerusalem. It was probably while still shepherding in the hills of Judea, long before he was king, that David wrote about his source of joy: "You have made known to me the path of life; you will fill me with joy in your presence" (Psalm 16:11).

Joy is also at the center of his most famous Psalm. "The Lord is my shepherd," David proclaims, and as he examines the implications of that, he writes: "my cup runneth over." The connection is made between relationship with God and joy.

Jesus completed this most famous, comforting figure of speech in all of literature when He called Himself the "good shepherd" and said His sheep listen to His voice and follow Him (John 10:14, 27). There is great joy when we will let Him, and no one else, be our Shepherd, leading us in "paths of righteousness."

David wrote in Psalm 1: "Blessed is the man who does not walk in the counsel of the wicked or stand in the way of sinners or sit in the seat of mockers." Someone has paraphrased that: "Blessed is the man who does not listen to him who is morally wrong." We are so prone to do that, and as a result, joy can leave. It left even David. Sometimes he stood "in the way of sinners." After he sins with Bathsheba, his joy is gone as he cries to God in familiar words. Most of us have confronted sin in our own lives and opened our Bibles to Psalm 51 and mourned with David:

> Cleanse me with hyssop, and I will be clean; wash

me, and I will be whiter than snow. Let me hear joy and gladness; let the bones you have crushed rejoice. . . . Do not cast me from your presence or take your Holy Spirit from me. Restore to me the joy of your salvation (Psalm 51:10-12).

Thankfully, we can pray Psalm 51 and then once again become those who do not "walk in the counsel of the wicked." Instead we can be those who "delight in the law of the Lord and meditate on it day and night." This meditating "day and night" is a key. The joyful Christian has searched out the truths of God in His word and then faithfully labored to implement them into his life. This is the reality of being led in "paths of righteousness."

Among the serious questions to ask ourselves is this one: will we live in the Spirit and revel in the Good Shepherd's protecting rod and His guiding staff? Many choose not to. Even some Christians begin thinking like a world who knows no shepherd. Humanistic thinking, with its doctrine of evolution and no supernatural God, leaves us free to select our own set of ethics and values. Self, often with little rationale other than "it feels good," makes its own rules, finds its own path. Self is god; self needs no shepherd.

And, as a result, daily, sin takes its toll. Two-year-old Bradley McGee dies of a brain hemorrhage "after his mother and stepfather punished him for soiling his diapers by repeatedly dunking him 'plunger-like' head-first into a commode."

Jim Bakker, handcuffed and shackled, is led

from his lawyer's office whimpering, "Please don't do this to me" (*The Joplin Globe*, 9/1/89, pp. 1A and 2C).

When I read of these things, and they are repeated countless times, I hear the psalmist light-years away from the empty, painful, whimpering paths of the world, pledging, "I will never forget your precepts for by them you have renewed my life," and I hear him singing, "Delight yourself in the Lord" (Psalm 119:93 and 37:4).

We should know the Shepherd so well, trust Him so completely, that we gladly follow and find that joy is a constant. Those who have followed find His mere existence delights and refreshes them. There are nights I have lain down to sleep and have remembered that the Lord is my shepherd, I have meditated on who He is, and I have been glad that I have let Him lead me, at least that day, in paths of righteousness. Often on those nights, as I am about to drift off to sleep, I have said to Him my shortest and most consistent prayer: "I love you." Every time I have said it (when my ring is safely on my finger and when it is not), He causes me to smile. And I have understood that only He is joy.

THE PROVISION OF GOD

After Jesus tells His disciples that they will be with Him again, He tells them another thing which is a component of joy: "My Father will give you whatever you ask in my name. . . . Ask and you will receive, and your joy will be complete" (John 16: 23-24). God will supply our needs; therefore, worry and fear can be replaced with joy.

This can be a fairly significant mystery. It's all we can do sometimes not to say, "Sure, Lord." How do we understand the promise "ask and ye shall receive, and your joy shall be complete" when Paul asked three times that a thorn in the flesh be removed? How do we understand "I shall not want" when Jesus Himself had nowhere to lay His head and when He "wanted" the cup removed?

I doubt we do understand without the continual awareness of our relationship with the Good Shepherd. "I shall not want" is filled with possibilities.

Perhaps we shall not want, because our desires are in keeping with the Spirit we have gladly yielded ourselves to. We have given up the pursuit of vain things. Those who shall not want no longer seek unimportant, even detrimental, riches and ease. No longer earth bound and short sighted, what we desire and ask for is to know the will and the ways of the Lord. We begin to have a relationship with the Father that makes us want what He wants. We know what things have value and what things don't.

Or maybe it means we have learned to be content, like Paul, in any situation. Would Paul have been more blessed if God had removed the thorn of the flesh instead of providing him with sufficient grace to cope? Which is the greater provision? God will give us what we really need. What we might perceive as adversity teaches us truths we would never have known otherwise. A martyr during the first centuries following Christ wrote this shortly before his death:

> In a dark hole I have found cheerfulness; in a place of bitterness and death I have found rest. While others weep I have found laughter, where others fear I have found strength. Who would believe that in a state of misery I have had great pleasure; that in a lonely corner I have had glorious company, and in the hardest bonds perfect repose. All these things Jesus has granted me. He is with me, comforts me and fills me with joy (Charles Hembree, *Fruits of the Spirit*, 32).

Tim Hansel, who suffers constant pain from a back injury, says that when he gets his frame of reference correct and his priorities straight, he understands what James means when he says to "consider it all joy": "Struggles pave the way to the gift of joy. They force us through the superficial crust of life to deeper inner peace. They are tools, you see, for discovering the deepest values that are in life and the deepest kind of joy that God gives" (*Holy Sweat*, 140). Hansel says that joy is "peace dancing."

But the main reason I have come to believe we can say with the psalmist, "I shall not want," is because we have the only things that really matter — peace with God for today and hope in Him for tomorrow. David knows God's comfort and healing when he declares: "He restoreth my soul."

Our souls are in such need of restoration. I have

stood in the shower after reading the morning newspaper and wept for the world. I have sat speechless at the ability of God's people to hurt one another. I have lain flat on my face before my God, repenting over my own sin. But in each of these desperate moments, I have remembered that the Shepherd does not desert His "cast sheep."

A cast sheep is an old English shepherd's term for a sheep who has turned over on his back and cannot get up again. The sheep, lying there struggling and bleating pathetically, will die if his owner does not arrive to help him in a reasonably short time (Philip Keller, *A Shepherd Looks at Psalm 23*). The Good Shepherd, though, counts His sheep and knows when one is missing or in trouble. He finds him and sets him back on his feet again. So the world may be sick, and God's people may hurt us because they are vulnerable and weak, and our own sin may disappoint us and God, but still He is our peace, there all through life to restore us.

He is, also, our hope. We who know and love the Shepherd can call even death, man's greatest foe, nothing but a shadow. The joy-filled Christian is not Dylan Thomas' speaker who bids us, "Do not go gentle into that good night," but "Rage, rage against the dying of the light." He is more like John Donne's confident speaker who mocks Death, giving him all kinds of reasons not to be proud, including the last and best one: "One short sleep past, we wake eternally / And death shall be no more; Death, thou shall die." We may walk as calmly and securely through the valley of the shadow of death, as we have walked through life. I will never forget the Christian father who wrote on the occasion of his 15-year-old son's death: "It is so painful to say goodbye; it will be so joyful to say, good morning, son." In death, the Shepherd will still be leading: "I will fear no evil, for you are with me."

Yes, my Joy, I shall never want. It is no wonder David exclaimed it — I exclaim it too: "And I shall dwell in the house of the Lord forever."

Chapter Twelve

Those Who Cry Out Can Sing

I never feel like I can ask God to help me in an endeavor unless I've done my part (how theologically sound that is, I do not know). Feeling like I do, you can be sure I practiced hard on the song I had been asked to sing. I thought I was quite ready to get up before the congregation and sing the "Sweet Hour of Prayer" Medley. Everything went fine for several measures. But during the second "sweet hour of prayer, sweet hour of prayer," I realized I had no idea what the next line was.

It is surprising what one can think of in a second or two. I ransacked my mind for the next line of the first verse and pondered why this was the only time I had forgotten it, I wondered how humming an interlude only eight words into the song would fly, I weighed the pro's and con's of stopping and starting again and thought how awful that would be. But most of all, I was amazed at how vulnerable I felt.

The happy ending to this story would be that the words came to me at the last tenth of a second, like they have done so often in the past. But this is not what happened. To my horror, the words never came, so I just grabbed some. (Some people get into this kind of challenge; I am not one of them.) First I picked a couple of lines from another verse; unfortunately, they were from the last verse, and I was on Mount Pisgah's lofty height, viewing my home and taking my flight. Where, pray tell, do you go from there? I had no idea. I ended up simply making up the last two lines, not one phrase at a time, but one painful word at a time. Incredibly, the two lines rhymed. I said something about being glad He was there — in the sweet hour of prayer. I wanted to die and thought the understatement fascinating when the medley moved right into "I Need Thee Every Hour." I need Him — every single second.

As the song ended and I made my way to my seat, I was in pretty bad shape. I'm ashamed to say that for one tiny second I actually wondered where God had been while I was standing up there trying to serve Him. I could see Him teaching me to do the best I can — if I had not practiced. I could see Him humbling me — if I hadn't learned that lesson long ago. But as far as I could figure, there was nothing to learn, so what was the deal? By the time I got home from church I had decided maybe it was just God's way of saying I might look into using other talents and packing this one away. Don't think I wasn't willing to oblige that Sunday.

When I broke my sullen silence to tell my husband what I was contemplating, he said he didn't even know anything was wrong when I sang and that I had never sung better. Oh, he noticed I had to wait a bit (three beats, I can tell you) to come in at one point, but he assured me the song brought glory to God. After some babying by a sweet husband, I decided maybe God didn't want me to quit singing.

I have never figured out what the purpose of that felt humiliation was. Maybe it was to show me that He provides in ways other than ways I anticipate, maybe it was to let me know the truth of the words "I Need Thee Every Hour" more greatly than I had every known them before. I don't know.

And I don't know why I felt somewhat betrayed over such a silly thing. But one thing that experience did is make me more sensitive to those who have felt, in very serious and lingering ways, truly betrayed by their God. I understand a little bit better why from time to time we find ourselves in situations that make us cry out: "My way is hidden from the Lord; my cause is disregarded by my God" (Isaiah 40:27).

When we are fired from a job or forced to retire from one we enjoy and "need," we might cry out.

When we are caught in the depths of clinical depression, we cry out.

When we sit across the desk from the doctor and hear the disease is irreversible and incurable, we cry out.

When we can't seem to free ourselves of some hateful, besetting sin, we cry out.

When our mate betrays us or doesn't want us anymore, we cry out.

When our babies die, we cry out.

For most of us there has been or will be a day to sit rocking and crying in the corner of a dark room or to lie desolate across our bed with our head buried in our hands. Many of us, even those of us with some faith, will cry out: "My way is hidden from the Lord; my cause is disregarded by my God." We will feel blasphemous, some of us, but we will say it. Where are you? Why don't you care about me? We turn to Isaiah 40, because it reminds us in verse 27 that that is often man's situation. We aren't the first to feel this way.

Captive Israel questions God, thinking He is neglecting them or has forgotten them. Isaiah, sent to be a comforting prophet to His discouraged people, has a message for the hopeless. Isaiah 40, his first address, must have been a great help for them. The last section, vv. 27-31, reveals much about man in his desperate hours and about his God.

What Isaiah says in response to the cry in v. 27 encouraged Israel to go on; it lets us get up and leave our dark room and go on, too.

First we are reminded of the God we think has deserted us. "Do you not know? Have you not heard?" Those who feel deserted and question God would have to have heard, would have to know. But they needed reminding, and so do we.

Isaiah appeals to their intelligence. Think. It isn't that God has forgotten them; they have forgotten God, or at least forgotten some things about God. They had been carried away into captivity, in part, because of their worship of idols. When they didn't acknowledge God as supreme, they became unable to see Him in creation and to learn of Him in the teaching that had been passed down to them.

So now, with great authority and confidence, God's prophet Isaiah reminds them: "The Lord is the everlasting God, the Creator of the ends of the earth. He will not grow tired or weary, and His understanding no one can fathom." Our God: always there, all powerful, all wise. They were thinking of Him in human terms. They needed to remember He is God. Jehovah does not faint from not eating or tire from not resting, like man does. If He has not acted, it is not because He is limited by anything, and it is not because He doesn't hear or care. They must not think they can understand His ways. Instead they must trust God to determine what to do and when to do it. God's people should trust Him in their darkness, because they have seen demonstrated, in so many ways, the truth about Him in the light.

Isaiah reminds the people of some of the truths about their God. He is everlasting while everything else in this mortal life is temporary. Many times that is the source of our pain. But the one who always was, who made evening and morning and "formed man from the dust of the ground and breathed into his nostrils the breath of life" (Genesis 1-2), is forever. He is also "the Creator of the ends of the earth" (Isaiah 40:28), who brings out the starry host one by one, and calls them each by name (v. 26). The creator cares for His creation, especially man, whom He made in His image.

His word tells us that He's always cared about His people. He is "the God of Abraham, the God of Isaac and the God of Jacob." This "God of people" appeared to Moses and stopped his excuses by asking "Who gave man his mouth?" He answers the question Himself: "Is it not I, the Lord? Now, go; I will help you speak and will teach you what to say."

This was the beginning of one man's understanding that God is always there. He was with him as he stood before Pharoah, as he walked through the Red Sea, as he left his tent and gathered quail and manna each morning — for forty years.

He was also with him when Moses may have come to his moment of "My cause is disregarded by my God." They had finally come to the edge of the Promised Land and were about to cross over. "O Sovereign Lord," he pleaded, ". . . Let me go over and see the good land beyond the Jordan — that fine hill country and Lebanon" (Deut.3:24-25). Moses once told the people of Israel of his plea and God's reply: "You shall not cross the Jordan" (Deut. 31:2). But even in his disappointment, as he turned the people over to the command of Joshua, he reminded them to "Be strong and courageous. Do not be afraid or terrified . . . for the Lord your God goes with you; he will never leave you nor forsake you" (Deut. 31:6).

Then scripture says, "Moses climbed Mount Nebo from the plains of Moab to the top of Pisgah, across from Jericho." And although he has said God will not forsake us, I wonder how it felt for Moses to turn and leave those he had led to the brink of the Promised Land. Did it feel like his "way was hidden from God"? Did his heart have trouble understanding what his mind believed?

But God was at the top of Mount Pisgah. He was there to show Moses the whole land. God was there to promise His friend Moses that that land would be given to his descendants. Perhaps as Moses and God shared this moment, Moses flashed back to a provision he'd only heard about — the day Pharoah's daughter had pulled him as a tiny, helpless baby out of a basket in the Nile. Leaving this earthly life behind would be no less poignant: God Himself buried his servant Moses, the prophet "whom the Lord knew face to face."

What Moses may not have understood in the desert east of the Jordan, he may have discerned at the top of Mount Pisgah: his way was never hidden from the Lord; his cause was never disregarded by an everlasting God, who never grows tired or weary, and whose understanding no one can fathom.

Isaiah, after describing our situation and reminding us of our God, tells us of the provision for "those who hope in the Lord."

What do we need most in our blackest hours? In any black hour, the main need is always the same. The man cleaning out his desk and closing his briefcase for the last time needs it. The woman sitting on the living room floor Indian style, dividing memories between her ex-husband and herself needs it. The widow eating another meal alone needs it. The husband who has promised his cancer-ridden wife he will tell her when it is very close to time for her to "go" needs it. That dying wife telling her husband and children goodbye needs it. The father and mother weeping at the graveside need it. The elderly church leader's wife trying to live again after being robbed and raped needs it. The sinner sitting on her back porch watching the rain fall through her tears needs it.

Isaiah 40:29 promises it. "He gives strength to the weary and increases the power of the weak." Faith is all that is needed to participate in this strength. The kind of person who hopes in the Lord, or "waits on the Lord" as the King James Version puts it, is one who shows his confidence in God's ability and willingness to execute His promises, by patiently awaiting their fulfillment (J. A. Alexander, *The Prophecies of Isaiah* 116). They hear God say as He said to Paul, "My grace is sufficient for you, for my power is made perfect in weakness" (II Cor. 12:9).

Each of us who hope in the Lord learns it, even if that hope is only a flicker, even if that hope is momentarily almost eclipsed.

Paula D'Arcy learned it in her dark hours. In her journal, *Song for Sarah*, she writes to her baby girl:

> Will you ever wonder what you were like when you were 16 months old? Well, today we danced magnificently before the stereo, laughing ourselves into one another.
> Each night before you go to sleep, I hold you and sing "Rock-a-bye, Baby." You'll never know how I feel, your curly head on my chest, as I hear you softly join in at the end.

After a tragic car accident takes the lives of this baby, Paula's husband, and their unborn child, Paula feels unable to go on. The journal entries that record her pain are simply too sad to read out loud. She didn't have energy for anything except to "stay alive and not scream." Hers is the anguish of those who feel their way is hidden from God.

Four months later, at Christmas, strength has come from somewhere, and she can believe that God loves her and that the only thing permanent in this world, in fact, is that love.

Six months after the accident, she records the

difficulty of the process of recovery and prays implicitly for strength:

> How easy it was to have what I called "faith" in our old life, with our walls full of love and our future full of promise. How easy, like loving someone who's only gentle and good. But this is hard faith now. How hard it is to believe that I am not alone with all this hurt. How hard it is to believe that there can be a victory the other side of these tears. But that is Christ's promise. I pray to find a way out of this. I want to get through it all.

Two and a half years later, she went to visit Sarah's grave and realized that she had found her way. She realized what she had put on Sarah's marker was true: "The Lord is my shepherd, I shall not want." "Over all is the hand of the shepherd," she writes. "Always for me, at every moment, he was there — there when I felt his presence, and equally there when it *seemed* I was alone." He had brought her through.

Isaiah gives us a clear perspective of what has been revealed about God and then reminds us we can draw on His strength. Once we do, we can walk again; we can even run. The picture in verse 31 is the antithesis of verse 27.

The cycle Isaiah describes, as old as mankind, is a miracle really. We feel God has deserted us and cry out, we remember our God, we pray for and receive His strength, and we find one day like Paula D'Arcy that "we are all quite safe." We find one day that we can sing and laugh again. We find one day that, metaphorically, our spirits soar.

It is also a miracle of sorts that those of us who have cried out "My way is hidden from the Lord" replace that declaration with another: "Thou art with me." We remember that He who told Isaiah to comfort His people, "speak tenderly" to His people, is with us. We can get up and leave the dark room. We also find that we love one scripture maybe beyond all others: "But those who hope in the Lord will renew their strength. They will soar on wings like eagles; they will run and not grow weary, they will walk and not be faint."

We love that verse, because we have claimed it. We have lived its wondrous truth.